GW00578319

BEYOND SURVIVAL

LIVING WELL IS THE BEST REVENGE

Yvonne Dolan

BT Press

A BT Press Book

First Published 1998 by Papier Maché Press (US) as *One Small Step*
First published in Great Britain 2000 by BT Press

Copyright © 1998 Yvonne Dolan

ISBN 1 871697 74 3

All rights reserved.
No part of this publication may be reproduced,
stored in a retrieval system, or transmitted, in any form
or by any means, without the prior permission
in writing of the publisher, nor be otherwise circulated
in any form of binding or cover other than
that in which it is published and without a similar condition
being imposed on the subsequent purchaser.

Typeset and Designed by Alex Gollner
Printed in England by Antony Rowe Ltd.

BT Press
17 Avenue Mansions
Finchley Road
London NW3 7AX
(020) 7794 4495

CONTENTS

Part One · Enjoying the Gifts of the Present

Part Two · Creating a Joyous Future

Part Three · Responding to Life's Challenges

Part Four · Support and Further Resources

To my mother,
Barbara Ogle Dolan Taylor,
with love and gratitude for our long ago walks
in the woods in the rain and so much more

A Personal Note to the Reader

Terrible things can happen in life with no warning, and afterwards we have no choice but to try to carry on as best we can. I learned this at a young age. My first memory as a young child is of a memorial service for my father. There I witnessed first-hand the emotional devastation wreaked by war: my mother's and grandparents' hearts and spirits were broken when my young father was killed in the Korean War.

Very early on I grieved that my father was gone from the world before I even knew him. Despite my mother's love and her desire to shield me from harm, I suffered multiple episodes of sexual and emotional abuse during my childhood. At these times I tried to comfort myself by imagining that if my father had lived he would have protected me from the abusers.

As I grew into adulthood, I struggled to come to terms with these and other bad things that happened and to embrace the good in the world around me in order to find strength to make my life worth living.

For people who have struggled with painful past events, and even for those who have not, *Beyond Survival* will unlock psychological resources and abilities you may never have realised you had, and empower you to create the life you want. I offer you this book as a talisman of hope and courage for your own journey and that of your clients. I affirm my faith in your ability to create the rewarding life you've always deserved. I did it, and believe me, you can do it too, beginning with one small step.

Wishing you all of life's blessings.

Yvonne Dolan

Foreword by
Harvey Ratner

Since it was founded in 1989, the Brief Therapy Practice has included international presentations as part of its programme of training events. Yvonne Dolan, a solution focused brief therapist and Ericksonian hypnotherapist from Denver, has proved time and time again to be one of our most popular speakers. She has that special ability to blend wisdom, humour and practicality with modesty and warmth, and it is a great pleasure to welcome her new book, which exhibits all these qualities in abundance.

Her 1991 publication, *Resolving Sexual Abuse*, is one of the most valuable contributions to the field, full of useful ideas and techniques for therapists helping those recovering from traumatic past events. I frequently raid her book for ideas (such as "the rainy day letter", one of her most famous techniques) for work with particular clients. Now I can turn to her new book, in which Yvonne refines some of her older techniques and introduces many new ones. It is a mine of information written in a clear, non-jargon style that makes it easy for anyone – clients and professionals alike – to use.

My regret is that *Beyond Survival* was not available a few years ago when I was facilitating groups for incest survivors. The chapter on support groups will be a rich resource for both clients and workers in providing exercises for group members, both individually and collectively, that will enhance the cohesion of the group and empower the individuals within it.

We have all waited a long time for Yvonne's follow-up to her earlier book, and have been amply rewarded for our patience.

Harvey Ratner
Brief Therapy Practice
London
September 2000

ACKNOWLEDGEMENTS

My mother, Barbara, to whom this book is dedicated, taught me to love books, defended me in grade school when a teacher mistook my extreme shyness for mental retardation, and insisted that I go to college at age eighteen even though I had no idea what I wanted to study.

Without the help of my agent, Leslie Breed, and the encouragement and kindness of my wonderful in-laws, Mary Ann and Gene Johnson, this book would not exist.

My husband, Charlie, helped me keep the faith when I was going through a series of hells including "book proposal hell", "title hell" and a few others for which I now have mercifully developed traumatic amnesia; he hugged me when I was profoundly discouraged; and took me out to dinner on numerous occasions when I had been too busy writing to remember to take anything out of the freezer. I love him more than words can say.

As with my previous book, my dear friends and colleagues Insoo Kim Berg and Steve de Shazer provided encouragement and professional inspiration through their books and work and, especially, by example.

The support and friendship of the following special people helped me endure what turned out to be a much longer writing project than anticipated: David Bice, Frank and Susan Bonomo, Bill and Evelyn Braithwaite, Marie-Christine Cabie, Louis Cauffman, Cheryl and Jeff Chang, Gene Combs, Mark and Julie Disorbio, Christine and Paul Drumwright, Jim Duval, Jill Freedman, Luc Isebaert, Miriam Le Fevre, Phyllis Firak Mitz, Kim Minor, Linda Mraz, Ruth Moorehouse, Denise Ross, Joan Robey, Katherine Lane Rossi, Karen Sands, Bob Schwartz, Steve Stajich and Jane Wingle.

Special thanks to David Schnarch whose books and conversations altered the way I view relationships, to Stephen Gilligan who has helped me to better understand the psychology of self relations, and to Ernest Rossi whose Ultradian concepts have transformed my work and lifestyle.

I especially want to thank my psychotherapy clients who have taught me so much and continue to do so.

Special thanks to the people who have sponsored my workshops and seminars and to all who have participated in them. Particular thanks to my colleagues and friends at the Korzybski Institute Brugge, the Korzybski Institute Holland, the Korzybski Institute Paris, the members of the European Brief Therapy Association, IACT, Bonomo & Bonomo, Chang & Chang, the Brief Family Therapy Center of Grand Rapids, the Justice Institute of British Columbia, the Milton Erickson Foundation, the Hinks Institute, the Brief Therapy Practice in London, the Brief Therapy Service at Centrecare in Perth, the Milton Erickson Institute of Chile, Centre de Psychotherapie Strategique in Montreal, the Suncoast Center of St Petersburg, the Milton Erickson Institute of Baltimore, the Maritime School of Social Work at Dalhousie University, ZIST, NIK in Bremen, NIK in Berlin, FKC in Stockholm, Klinik St Martin, the Family Institute of Maine, the Family Therapy Networker, and the Richmond Veterans Hospital.

PREFACE

As I write this preface to the new British edition of Beyond Survival, yet another war rages in eastern Europe leaving many people homeless and grieving the loss of loved ones, others carrying painful memories and physical scars from the violence they suffered. Newspapers, television and radio broadcasts continue to document the alarming frequency of sexual and physical abuse, domestic violence, hate crimes and other acts of senseless cruelty in our modern world.

At times such as this, I am reminded of the long-ago advice of my grandmother: "It's better to light even a little candle than to curse the darkness." Grandmother understood the practicality and efficacy of small steps. This book is my attempt to light a "little candle".

Terrible things can and do happen every day to good people and afterwards there is little choice but to try to carry on as best we can. Ironically, life itself is often the most effective cure. In order to move beyond the negative effects of trauma, loss, abuse and other painful past experiences, the present needs to become more vivid and compelling than the past, and we need to recover the ability to hope and dream about the future and to take practical action towards making those dreams come true.

While nothing can erase past traumas, creating a rewarding life in the present so that it becomes more figural and vivid than the past can help counterbalance the terrible things that happen in life and take away much of their power. Sometimes the first and most significant step towards making the present more figural than the past is realising that your are not alone in suffering.

Telling the details of painful past events to a supportive listener can provide validation, support and release from shame. While this constitutes an important step in recovering from the effects of trauma, unfortunately it is simply not enough. Furthermore, continuing to dwell on painful details of trauma or abuse over extended time can exacerbate symptoms of anxiety and depression and contribute to a "victim" mindset of passivity ("Why bother, nothing good ever happens to me") and learned helplessness ("There's nothing I can do to make things better"). Often something more is needed. I wrote this book to provide exactly that.

Recorded between the lines of this book is my own journey as well as that of my psychotherapy clients, family and friends who inspired me by their courage and determination to create lives that now shine brightly.

Early on in my own life, I endured the death of my father and multiple episodes of sexual and emotional abuse. As I grew into adulthood, I struggled to come to terms with these and other bad things that happened and to embrace the good in the world around me in order to find strength to make my life worth living.

For people who have struggled with painful past events, and even for those who have not, Beyond Survival will unlock psychological resources and abilities you may have never realised you possessed and empower you to create the life you want. I offer you this book as a talisman of hope and courage for your own journey and that of people who are dear to you. I affirm my faith in your ability to create the rewarding life you've always deserved. I did it and believe me, you can do it too, beginning with one small step.

Yvonne Dolan
September 30, 2000

Introduction
Moving Beyond
Survivorhood

"If I had my life to live over, I would start barefoot
earlier in the spring and stay that way later in the fall.
I'd go to more dances, I'd ride more merry-go-rounds.
I'd pick more daisies."

– Nadine Stair, age eighty-five

"It's Time to Get on With My Life"

Maggie slumped on the couch in my office, fingers fidgeting in her jacket
pocket, searching for the cigarettes she had given up several months ago.
Her eyes were red from crying, and her voice trembled as she spoke.

> I've spent my whole life getting over what happened to me. I keep
> trying and trying to make a good life for myself, a happy life, but it
> never works out the way I hoped. I've done all the things you're
> supposed to do to survive being abused as a kid, and to get over
> the other bad things that happened later. I'm 32 years old, and I'm
> tired of waiting. When am I going to start enjoying my life?

Maggie's awareness that she needs to move beyond surviving the past
and start living a rewarding life, and her frustration at feeling stuck in her
efforts to do so, reflect the experience of many people I have seen in my
psychotherapy practice over the past twenty-three years.

The answer to Maggie's question is *now*. I wrote this book for people
who have endured traumas and now want to get on with living their own
lives. If you have survived pain - physical, sexual or emotional abuse,
divorce or relationship difficulties, illness or accidents, loss, or other

traumatic life experiences – and want to finally live with joy, this book is for you.

Beyond Survival is especially intended for the person who is willing, but at times finds it difficult, to embrace the future with joy. It is an invitation to create the kind of future that you want to live, regardless of what happened or was done to you in the past. If you are wondering whether this applies to you, ask yourself this question: "Why settle for anything less?"

Maggie is not only going to start living her own life, she is also going to give herself a good life, a life that authentically reflects the self she was born to be: she will restore her capacity to experience joy.

SMALL STEPS TO A REWARDING LIFE

Regardless of what happened in the past, you can begin to create a rewarding and satisfying life for yourself now. This book will guide you through the process of creating the life you've been wanting, one small step at a time. As you progress through the chapters, your hopes and dreams will gradually become far more vivid and compelling than your past experiences, resulting in a restored sense of wonder and joy in living that you may have once feared was gone forever. Approaching cherished hopes and dreams one small step at a time makes them less daunting and, most importantly, makes them undeniably achievable in everyday life.

WHY VIEWING YOURSELF AS A SURVIVOR IS NOT ENOUGH

I originally decided to write this book because I was troubled by the emergence of a "survivor culture" in America. In attempting to respond to the very real and pervasive phenomenon of victimisation, the psychotherapy profession inadvertently created a "survivor identity".

I do not believe this phenomenon has occurred because past ideas about what helps people recover from abuse and other traumas were necessarily wrong. Rather, it has occurred because psychotherapists have not yet extended ideas about recovery far enough to help people move beyond Survivorhood. Overcoming the immediate effects of abuse, loss or other trauma and viewing yourself as a Survivor rather than a Victim, are helpful steps, but are ultimately not sufficient to help people fully regain the ability to live a life that is more compelling, joyous and fulfilling than your past.

While many self-help books have documented the painful effects of victimisation and the value of recognising oneself as a survivor, no one warned us about the negative consequences that can result from continuing to think of oneself over an extended period of time primarily as a survivor.

Unfortunately the "survivor" mind-set that people typically develop to get through painful past experiences can later interfere with their capacity to fully enjoy life. People who embrace "survivor" as their primary identity over the long-term by necessity tend to filter experiences of daily living through two criteria: how a current event resembles or differs from the traumatic event that happened in the past, and a current experience mitigates or worsens the continuing effects of the past trauma.

As a result, people who remain at the Survivor stage see life through the window of their Survivorhood rather than enjoying the more immediate and unconstricted vision of the world with which they were born. Such a limited view diminishes the ability to experience, much less enjoy the moment. This inability to truly appreciate your present life can also interfere with the capacity to fully enjoy a healthy and rewarding sexual relationship with a partner.

The idea that continuing to think of oneself primarily as a survivor over an extended period of time was not helpful first occurred to me in the late 1980s when a puzzling phenomenon was described by numerous North American psychotherapists attending my seminars on treatment of sexual abuse and other traumas.

Many of their patients who described themselves as "survivors" (of abuse) over an extended period of time seemed to be suffering from a low-grade depression, and expressed pessimism about the possibility for happiness in the future. Furthermore, these patients complained that they found themselves constantly evaluating the present in comparison with the things they had survived in the past, and that they had trouble enjoying themselves in the moment.

Later, in 1995, I noticed a phenomenon that suggested that moving beyond thinking of oneself as a survivor could be a valuable step. I had just begun interviewing people for a small pilot study exploring the characteristics of people who had suffered sexual abuse earlier in life and were now living healthy, satisfying lives characterised by enduring relationships, meaningful work and an absence of debilitating psychiatric symptoms.

Of the twenty people I interviewed, not one of them used the words "victim" or "survivor" to describe how they currently viewed themselves. I was not surprised at the absence of the word, "victim", since by definition these were people who had managed to get beyond their victimisation in terms functioning in life. But I was puzzled by the absence of "survivor" in their responses to questions about how they thought of themselves.

When I asked the various interviewees what they thought about the "survivor" label, there was a striking consistency in their responses. They told me, "Yes, I survived what happened to me, but that's not who I am now," or "That's not how I think of myself now." Or they answered, "I haven't thought about myself that way for a long time," or "Well, that's part of me, but that's not *all* of who I am," and other similar responses.

In contrast, many of the people seeking my help as a psychotherapist seemed to be experiencing the phenomenon described by the psychotherapists attending my seminars. Repeatedly they told me, "I'm a survivor of sexual abuse [or physical abuse, or emotional abuse, or other trauma] and I've done all the right things the books say we're supposed to do to get over it, but I'm still not happy."

These people were not lazy or what doctors sometimes call malingerers. They were genuinely and earnestly trying to get on with their lives. And like Maggie, they were frustrated as hell. It gradually dawned on me that in creating the label of "survivor", the psychotherapy field had created the potential for a new set of problems.

THE OLD STAGES AND THE NEW ONE

As a psychotherapist interning at a telephone crisis centre in the 1970s, I was taught that there were two stages of recovery from traumas involving emotional, physical or sexual abuse, and other life events. The Victim Stage is necessarily the beginning of healing. When you first face the reality of a bad thing that was done to you or the bad thing(s) that happened to you, you begin to acknowledge the feelings (usually grief and anger) that accompany this.

Allowing yourself to feel these emotions and express them is a vital part of the healing process and a valuable aspect of the Victim Stage. Furthermore, realising that you have been victimised implies that you recognise that what happened was not your fault. Recognising that you have been a victim of circumstances or other people serves the important purpose of allowing you to let go of self-blame and shame. Another aspect of recognising yourself as a victim is finding the courage to tell someone else what happened to you.

Telling your story to a compassionate listener breaks down the isolation that causes fear and shame. You are no longer alone with the bad thing that happened or was done to you. The only disadvantages of the Victim Stage are those that occur if a person continues to identify with the Victim Identity beyond its usefulness.

Once you have identified and expressed the feelings that resulted from being victimised, broken down the isolation by telling a caring person what happened to you and realised that you are not to blame for the abuse or other bad things that were done to you, the Victim label has done its work.

Continuing to think of yourself primarily as a Victim beyond that point can eventually lead to feelings of helplessness, despair and a resulting passivity that can make you vulnerable to further victimisation. As soon as you realise that you are not to blame for the bad thing(s) that happened, it is time to began to recognise yourself as a Survivor.

The Survivor Stage begins when you understand that you have lived beyond the time at which the traumatic experience occurred. Thinking of yourself as a survivor has many advantages. "Survivor" undeniably reinforces the fact that the abuse or other traumatic event is in the past.

Realising that you survived leads to wondering, "How did I do it? How was I was able to survive this?" Acknowledging that you are a Survivor invites you to develop an inventory of the positive personality characteristics that allowed you to survive what happened, to identify and appreciate the internal strengths (knowledge, courage, spirituality or other positive aspects of yourself) and external resources (friends, supportive family members, community support) that you already possessed at the time of the trauma or developed afterwards in order to survive it.

A significant hallmark of the Survivor Stage is that you regain your ability to function productively in everyday life. A Survivor is able to focus on daily activities such as work, childcare, household duties, community activities, hobbies and spending time with friends.

Once you recognise that you have lived past the occurrence of the traumatic event and you acknowledge and appreciate the strengths and resources that have allowed your survival and eventual well-being, the Survivor Identity has done its work. For people who remain at this stage permanently, life is constantly filtered through the window of their Survivorhood. All events are evaluated in terms of how they resemble, differ from, mitigate or worsen the effects of the past. This diminishes the ability to fully experience and enjoy life and is, I believe, responsible for the "flatness" and low-grade depression reported by so many self-described Survivors of sexual abuse and other painful life events.

As Clarissa Pinkola Estes explains in her wonderful book, *Women Who Run With the Wolves*:

> If we stay as survivors only, without moving to thriving, we limit ourselves and cut our energy to ourselves and our power in the world to less than half.

Estes goes on to suggest that rather than becoming a permanent primary identity, Survivor needs ultimately to become "one of many badges" that you wear, a source of pride but not the determinant of your identity. Survivor is not an aspect of yourself that should be discarded, but rather appreciated as a significant aspect of yourself. Embraced in this way, surviving the trauma you endured in the past is an accomplishment that you can continue to celebrate without suffering negative consequences. Furthermore, this will allow you to move on and create the life you so richly deserve.

Recently, I have been heartened to hear psychotherapists and people in support groups echoing the need for people to move beyond thinking of themselves primarily as Survivors. In some psychotherapy circles this next phase has been referred to as a "Thriver" Stage. While defined vaguely until now, the notion of a third stage indicates that people are beginning to realise that more research is needed.

In thinking about this third stage, I have struggled with what to call it. Initially I liked the term "Thriver" because of its positive connotation. But it rhymes with "Survivor", which may have negative connotations for people who are trying to leave behind painful memories.

Then it dawned on me. In retrospect, it seems obvious: the third stage is the stage in which you become fully, joyously and authentically yourself. You begin living not only in reference to the bad things you survived or even in reference to present experiences and hopes for the future, but according to the totality of who you really are as a person deep inside. You become completely yourself and enjoy the rewards of doing so.

The Authentic Self Identity allows you more freedom than either of the preceding roles. Thinking of yourself in this way will allow you to experience a more compelling present and contemplate a future that is more vivid and fulfilling than your past.

You will be able to enjoy life to the fullest, exulting in experiences that reach the potential you were born with, expressing yourself in the most personally rewarding and creative ways available to you as you go through your every day life. Your current experiences and relationships will increasingly evoke a sense of immediacy, wonder and an enhanced potential for growth.

So what could be disadvantageous about identifying with your Authentic Self, embracing your own potential to fully experience life and express all the gifts you were born with? While the drawbacks are minimal to the advantages, it is only fair to state them. When initially connecting or re-connecting with your Authentic Self, this new way of thinking may feel unfamiliar and therefore uncomfortable.

Over time as you continue to live in harmony with your Authentic Self, lifestyle, relationships and life decisions may be less predictable and more complex than they were when you primarily identified with the Survivor or Victim images. From the vantage point of your Authentic Self, you should become increasingly secure with and trusting of your own knowledge and abilities. Consequently you may become less invested in maintaining the status quo in your life, and therefore less willing to squander your time and energy on relationships or situations that have become abusive or toxic for you. Instead you will devote your time and energy to the life you truly want and deserve.

How to Use This Book

This book can be used in several ways: as a series of mental exercises, or as a daily or weekly format for your personal journal. You can record your responses to the exercises on paper or on audiotape, or just think about your responses if you prefer.

No matter how you chronicle your responses, the most important result of continuing to take small steps towards alignment with your Authentic Self will be the rewarding changes that allow you to confidently pursue your hopes and dreams.

This book is divided into four parts. The first part, Enjoying the Gifts of the Present, is dedicated to exploring and expressing your Authentic Self. Chapter One, Getting to Know Your Authentic Self, is devoted to exploring, identifying and appreciating who you really are deep inside, beyond whatever bad things happened to you in the past. Chapter Two, Welcome Home!, invites you to develop new ways to express and enjoy yourself at home. Chapter Three, Enjoying Yourself More at Work, offers ideas for making the work environment a place that enhances rather than detracts from your quality of life.

Part Two, Creating a Joyous Future, invites you to reclaim cherished hopes and dreams, to begin making them realities and to create time to enjoy the results. Chapter Four, Hopes and Dreams and Miracles, guides you through identifying what you really want from your life now. Chapter Five, Yes, You Can!, offers strategies for transforming seemingly impossible or daunting goals into realistic possibilities. Chapter Six, Time on Your Hands, provides ideas for changing how time affects your ability to realise goals and enjoy your everyday life.

Part Three, Responding to Life's Current Challenges, helps you identify what really works best for you when people, memories from the past or demands of the present threaten the gains you've made in creating the life you deserve. Chapter Seven, Partners, Parents, Kids and Extended Family, provides guidelines to help you identify ways to be creative, flexible and true to yourself while responding to the needs of the people you love. Chapter Eight, Coping when the Past Rears its Ugly Head, offers ways to limit or permanently resolve residual effects of post-traumatic stress in your life. Chapter Nine, Dealing with Rainy Days and Dark Nights, provides sensible coping strategies for getting through the "blues" that occur occasionally as a by-product of living a heartfelt life.

Part Four, Support and Further Resources, helps you maintain the momentum you've built up as you've progressed through the earlier sections of the book by inviting you to connect with supportive, like-minded people in person or through literature. Chapter Ten, How to Start a Small Steps Support Group, supplies the specifics you need to start and continue an ongoing group of people dedicated to supporting one another's exploration and positive expression of life beyond Survivorhood.

A Suggested Reading List offers a selection of books you may want to read for further exploration. Finally, there are blank pages in which to record important thoughts and insights that occur to you as you continue to pursue and develop a good life for yourself.

Origins of the Techniques in this Book

Beyond Survial is not intended as a substitute for psychotherapy; however, the exercises throughout have been carefully designed according to psychotherapeutic principles in order to evoke feelings of comfort and reassurance, and to empower the reader to identify, explore and expand her own unique solutions to the "problem" of creating a joyous, healthy and rewarding life in the future that extends beyond Survivorhood.

The exercises in this book are derived from the principles and psychotherapy techniques of Solution-Focused Therapy (Berg, Miller, de Shazer, Lipchik, Nunally, Molnar, Gingerich, Weiner-Davis, Furman, Ahola, O'Hanlan).

Basic to this approach is the concept of the client and therapist co-creating solutions by client and therapist (O'Hanlon and Weiner-Davis, 1989.) This idea is based on the respectful assumption that psychotherapy clients have highly individualised and uniquely effective solutions to the problems that bring them to therapy, and that these solutions can be elicited through therapists asking meaningful questions. Solution-focused therapy assumes the construction of a solution is a joint process between client and therapist, with the therapist taking responsibility for empowering the client to create and experience her own uniquely meaningful and effective therapeutic changes. This posture of respect, pragmatism and hopefulness is uniquely suited to people who have survived physical, emotional and sexual abuse and other traumas.

While consistent with solution-focused concepts, the Ericksonian Relaxation Method in Chapter One and the Symbol for the Time of Your Life centreing technique in Chapter Six are derived in part from the psychotherapeutic principles of Ericksonian Utilisation. Closely related to the solution-focused approach, Ericksonian Utilisation was developed by the psychiatrist Milton Erickson.

The Ericksonian Utilisation approach is based on the principle that psychotherapy clients' already existing perceptions, life experiences, behaviours and personality traits are potentially valuable resources that may be incorporated into the therapeutic change process for the purpose of relieving symptoms and improving quality of life.

The Utilisation concept implies that every part of the person's behaviour, personality traits, relationships, personal beliefs and values is potentially valuable and useful in enabling them to achieve more rewarding choices and experiences in life. Based on this concept, the Ericksonian relaxation exercises I include in this book invite the client to utilise aspects of previous moments in every day life in which she has felt comfortable, centred and relaxed in order to re-elicit these feelings when needed in the present.

My own work as a psychotherapist in treating survivors of sexual abuse and other traumas using Solution-Focused Therapy and Ericksonian approaches is documented in *Resolving Sexual Abuse: Solution-focused and Ericksonian Hypnosis for Adult Survivors* (1991, Norton), and in various journal articles and book chapters. I have been training psychotherapists in Solution-Focused techniques for ten years, and conduct seminars at universities, hospitals and mental health centres throughout the US and Canada and in Europe, South America, Australia and Asia.

And Now to Begin

I am inviting you to make a commitment - not to me, or to this book, but to yourself. I suggest that you devote at least one hour a week to implementing the ideas described in this book. Certainly, you may decide to spend more time, but even an hour a week will yield results. Change is inevitable. Our goal here is to increase the percentage of changes that happen in your life that are to your liking, and to empower you to create the changes you desire through series of inviting small steps that you'll want to do.

I realise that by the time you are reading these words, you may have been badly battered by life, and may be experiencing the cynicism and despair that sometimes result. Nevertheless, the meaning of these words applies to you. (I assure you, it does!) Step by step you will build or reclaim the life for which you secretly long, a life beyond the past that joyously and completely reflects who you really are.

PART ONE

·

ENJOYING
THE GIFTS OF THE PRESENT

Chapter One
Getting to Know
Your Authentic Self

When what we do grows out of inner conviction that
whatever it may be that we choose to do in a moment
or in our lifetime is meaningful, there is soul in the
choice.

–Jean Shinoda Bolen

I saw a strikingly handsome Japanese tea bowl that
had been broken and pieced together. The image of
that bowl made a lasting impression. Instead of trying
to hide the flaws, the cracks were emphasized, filled
with silver. The bowl was even more precious after it
had been mended.

–Sue Bender

Imagine that you have just found out that you own a wonderful home on
a beautiful estate. The house reflects your special and unique values and
tastes, and the climate there is in beautiful harmony with your moods.

You have owned this wonderful acreage and the home within it all your
life, since earliest childhood, but at some point you were forced to move
away from it. It may have been a long while since you have visited your
lovely home and delighted in the beautiful grounds, trees and flowers and
other well-cared-for living things in the surrounding acreage.

You may have forgotten what your house and estate look like, or even
that you own it. Perhaps you were told long ago (wrongly!) that the house
and its beautiful grounds no longer belonged to you. Or maybe, early in
childhood, you were given the message that you could no longer live there

if you wanted to be loved by your parents or other caregivers. Regardless of any messages sent to you by other people, this estate always has and always will belong to you and you alone. The estate, and the wonderful home it contains, is your Authentic Self.

It is now time to return and re-acquaint yourself with your personal estate - your Authentic Self - so you can fully experience all of its rewards and delights. You'll know you are truly reunited with your Authentic Self when your life is infused with wonder and joy. Welcome home!

What is your Authentic Self? In times of emotional calm, it is your psychological sanctuary deep within, a place where you can heal your wounds, explore and embrace the deeper longings of your heart and take delight in the experience of being alive.

In times of crisis or intense emotional experiences, your Authentic Self is an island of safety and constancy that remains solid and intact, like a lighthouse beaconing reassuringly beyond the ravages of winds and stormy seas. Your Authentic Self exists beyond the weather of our constantly changing emotions, thoughts and opinions. It is:

> That "you" (that is) the unchanging presence or permanent "I" that witnesses all of the changing "I's," i.e., I feel good, I feel bad, I like you, I don't like you. (Wolinsky, 1996)

This chapter is organised into three sections designed to help you move into the estate of your Authentic Self. The first section will strengthen and replenish you as you explore your Authentic Self through words. The next section will assist you in creating a symbolic representation of your Authentic Self. The final section, which focuses on relaxation and play, will guide your exploration of your inner resources through a powerful self-relaxation technique and a "date" or mini-vacation with your Authentic Self.

If these activities initially strike you as frivolous or self-indulgent, remember that loving, exploring and honouring the person you really are deep inside will further develop and enhance your capacity to love and nurture others as well as yourself. When you suffer an inability to love and appreciate yourself, you are equally unable to fully love another person.

Exploring Your Authentic Self through Words

Through creative writing we learn a surprising number of things about ourselves. The following will amaze and delight you with personal insights, re-enforcing your sense of value and reminding you of the special characteristics you bring into the world.

Keeping a Journal

I strongly encourage you to purchase a journal for yourself. Having one place in which to record your thoughts, ideas, observations and responses to the exercises in this book will support the importance of your work exploring your Authentic Self. A journal is an ongoing gift to yourself. Daily entries ensure a continuing dialogue with your Authentic Self.

If you find that you have little to say on some days, don't worry. This does not signify a lack of progress, but is a normal occurrence among journal writers. Feeling empty of your own words may mean you are ready to absorb more learning from other people.

Perhaps you have heard the proverbial story of the pilgrim who visits a famous teacher, hoping to learn from him. The teacher asks the pilgrim to pour him a cup of tea, instructing him: "I will tell you when to stop." To the pilgrim's horror, the teacher says nothing and the tea spills over the cup and splashes on the floor.

Finally the teapot is empty and the pilgrim places it on the table. The teacher tells him: "You are like that teacup. You are so full you cannot take in anything more. You must first empty yourself if you wish to learn from me."

Days when your journal entry is rich and full can be exciting and satisfying. At the same time, it is important to appreciate the gift of days when your word cup is empty and you are open to the words of others.

There are probably as many approaches to journal writing as there are personality styles, and this is reflected in myriad books on the topic. If you are looking for a book to help you explore and develop your journal style, I recommend Lucia Capacchione's wonderful book *The Creative Journal*.

Identifying the activities and every day experiences that you most enjoy and appreciate is a pleasant way to begin exploring and strengthening your connection to your Authentic Self.

Just now as I was writing this, I realised that one of the treasured experiences I had not indulged in for a long time was taking a leisurely walk through the Denver Botanical Gardens near my home. My favourite part of the gardens is an Alpine exhibit complete with miniature versions of Arctic poppies, tiny cactus and exquisite diminutive wildflowers that grow at high altitudes.

While my morning started out on a hectic note, thinking about visiting that little Alpine garden had a replenishing effect. I could actually feel my shoulders relaxing at the thought of the Lilliputian daisies and wild purple lilies framed by distant snow-covered peaks against a bright blue sky. Just thinking about the things (or people) you love can sometimes be nourishing as it helps you reconnect with your Authentic Self.

The things you especially enjoy doing or experiencing are like little holograms, self-contained images of who you really are deep inside. Identifying these and subsequently reconnecting to them in thought or action will simultaneously strengthen your awareness and appreciation of your Authentic Self. And, if you happen to be weary from too many outside obligations, worries and chores of daily life, as I was earlier today, doing this exercise will refresh you.

A Pleasant Journey to Your Memory Bank

 One Small Step

Imagine that you have been given the opportunity to spend the next fifteen minutes in your personal Memory Bank reliving one or more pleasant or meaningful experiences you have enjoyed over the last year. What experience or experiences would you choose to relive? Take a few moments now to enjoy reliving one of these experiences in your mind, savouring what you most enjoyed, and noticing what appeals to you about it.

 Possibilities

Which experiences would you choose to relive? (If you have trouble summoning up positive experiences you would like to recur, try identifying those you would least dislike repeating.)

When considering experiences you would value repeating in your life, it is important to include those occurrences you have enjoyed infrequently, as well as those you encounter on a day to day basis.

I asked Erin, a busy mother of two young children, what experiences and activities she especially valued and wanted to have continue in her life. Here are a few of the things she said:

> "I like to watch sunsets from our living room window. I like to give my baby a bath. He loves the water and his smile melts me. I like to go to High Tea at the Brown Palace. I like to spend time alone with my husband."

Although some of Erin's experiences happen more frequently in her life than others, all of the above are representations of the Authentic Erin, meaningful reflections of who she really is. Furthermore, even when she doesn't have time to engage in her favourite activities, thinking about them helps her connect with her sense of self.

You may want to carry this list with you so you can reread it whenever you want. It can serve as a mental bridge to the resources and potential comfort inherent in your Authentic Self as you manage daily responsibilities. This is particularly useful when you are under stress or when painful memories or fears about the future interfere with your ability to enjoy the present.

A Message from a Guardian Angel

Imagine that a wise and compassionate guardian angel has been sitting on your shoulder since you were born. You have not been aware of this presence up until now because angels are weightless. The angel's sole purpose has been to recognise and observe all your positive personality strengths and virtuous beliefs about the world. This is not an angel in charge of producing self criticism or blame!

One Small Step

For the next fifteen minutes, imagine that the angel is now dictating a list of your positive attributes through you. Writing down whatever comes to mind, make a list of what you think the angel would say.

Possibilities

Which personality traits do you most value and wish to continue influencing your approach to life?
Which virtues or positive beliefs do you most value and wish to continue influencing your approach to life?

Once you have completed this exercise, take some time to contemplate what you wrote. What was it like creating the list? Perhaps, even with the device of the imaginary guardian angel, you found it difficult to catalogue your positive personality characteristics. If so, don't worry, this is not uncommon, particularly if you come from a family or culture where such self-acknowledgment is not encouraged.

Try imagining what worthwhile and good things another person who understands you would notice about you. Or you might find it more helpful to imagine what good things an understanding and kindly stranger would notice while watching a videotape of your life. And be sure to start the list by noting your modesty! Once you have created the list, take a moment to consider any attributes or virtue you may have overlooked.

A bright and gifted scientific researcher who had taught at two universities, Belinda found herself stumped when she first attempted to imagine an angel dictating a list of her positive personality qualities. Naming positive qualities seemed too much like "blowing her own trumpet", a form of conceit that in her childhood she had been taught was wrong.

In the Irish Catholic family where Belinda grew up, people who talked too highly about themselves were considered braggarts, and were ridiculed as being "full of themselves." Furthermore, people who viewed themselves as pious or holy were considered to be self-righteous phonies. For Belinda, imagining an angel saying positive things about her was egotistical and felt like boasting.

Despite ridiculing any form of self-praise, Belinda's family advocated complimenting other people, especially those who were absent or lived outside the immediate family circle.

As a result, a more comfortable and acceptable way for Belinda to identify positive personality traits in herself was to imagine the words that a caring friend might use to describe her. By imagining what her best friend Sarah might say, Belinda came up with the following list:

> Belinda has a good sense of humour.
> Belinda is careful and conscientious in her work.
> Belinda is a loyal friend.

If, like Belinda, identifying positive personality traits about yourself was initially difficult or uncomfortable, chances are you were taught in childhood that directly expressing positive feelings about yourself was unacceptable. Or perhaps you suffered psychological abuse and were thereby given the message that you did not deserve to feel good about yourself. Regardless of the cause, having difficulty identifying and acknowledging positive qualities and characteristics about yourself indicates that it is time to reclaim this ability.

The next exercise will help you to identify some of your philosophy and beliefs about life that characterise your Authentic Self. This exercise is adapted from *Writing for Your Life* by Deena Metzger.

The Last Fifteen Minutes of the World
Imagine that you have been gifted at birth with two things: the ability to express yourself well, and some special knowledge to give the world. Unfortunately, you have not known of these abilities until now. You have also just learned that a terrible destructive force is about to hit the earth. This destructive force will destroy all libraries, museums, computers and other information storage systems. Only those objects and information placed in a special time capsule will survive.

 One Small Step
You have been asked to contribute to the time capsule. Write, draw

or tape your special information that will help the human race to survive afterwards. You have only fifteen minutes to do this.

It is important that you limit yourself to just fifteen minutes so that the process is spontaneous and does not become laboured. It is also a good idea for you to preserve your response in some way, so that you can take time afterwards to explore what the words tell you about your Authentic Self at this juncture in your life.

No two responses to this exercise will be alike. Since your Authentic Self is constantly growing, changing and evolving, your responses are likely to vary on different occasions. Here is a portion of the response I wrote while writing this book:

> We must remember to expect, anticipate and notice the inevitable good things, small or large, that also happen as part of daily life. It is better to live a life focused upon and influenced by the awareness of those good things than the fear of the bad things.

Remember that there is no "wrong" response to this exercise. It is also important to allow yourself to respond with humour if that is what you feel when doing the exercise.

When participating in one of my workshops, Ron found himself laughing aloud because the first thing he had written for the imaginary time capsule was: "Don't sit in the Poison Ivy." He had thoughtfully illustrated this suggestion with a drawing of the little three-leafed poisonous plant.

Not sitting in Poison Ivy was eminently sensible advice, and when he considered it on a metaphorical level, Ron found it was an important reminder from his Authentic Self about the need to pay attention to the obvious in life, something he had been neglecting recently. Whatever your response to the exercise, appreciate what it tells you about the beliefs and philosophy of your Authentic Self.

Telling Your Life Story

Writing or taping your autobiography is another way to explore and deepen a connection with your Authentic Self. Depending on the amount of detail you want to include, creating your story may take hours, days, weeks or longer. After you have written it, read it again, and add details, until you are satisfied that you have included everything that is important to you.

In writing your story, beware of perfectionism! Remember that the purpose is to learn more about your Authentic Self by describing the events and experiences that are significant to you. Some people find it easier to write an autobiography if they start by focusing on a particular theme such as "Houses I Have Lived In", "Important People In My Life", "Schools I Attended", "Pets I Have Loved", "Trips I Have Taken", "Treasured Friendships" or other significant topics.

If you are having a hard time beginning, despite focusing on a theme, you might like to try the following exercise.

 One Small Step
Give yourself three minutes to tell the story of your life. After three minutes, take note of what you have written and decide whether you want to continue for another three minutes.

Because it is a near impossible and slightly absurd task, this exercise often loosens the constrictions of self-imposed perfectionism and allows your Authentic Self to speak more freely.

A Time Line
If you wish to tell your story but do not want to do it as a narrative, try creating a Time Line.

 One Small Step
1. Draw a vertical line down the middle of a sheet of paper. On the upper left hand corner write the word "birth" and your date of birth. Now, in chronological order, list other pieces of information about yourself, such as approximate dates of starting school, moving house, birth of siblings and so on. Add information as it comes to you, including both pleasant and unpleasant information that feels significant.
2. Record past or current feelings about each event in the space opposite it on the right-hand side of the vertical line.

One page will probably not be enough. You may want to cut the paper horizontally and use cellotape and additional strips of paper in order to insert additional information in chronological order. Some people like to use paper and tape to form one long strip of paper which they then roll up and store in the form of a long scroll.

CREATING A SYMBOL
FOR YOUR AUTHENTIC SELF

Words are not the only way to explore and connect more completely to your Authentic Self. Some people find it more meaningful to create a symbol or series of symbols that help them to identify, explore and further develop who they really are deep within.

A Coat of Arms

If you were to create a Coat of Arms to represent your Authentic Self which images would you include? Which colours best represent who you are? Would you include things that represent your accomplishments, your hobbies and other things you like to do? Is there a saying or a logo that you would include in the form of an inscription or a banner? Notice what comes to mind.

Brad was just doodling when he began his Coat of Arms. He was sitting in a café waiting for a friend, and found himself playfully drawing the image of a feather on the back of his notebook.

Brad then found himself drawing another feather, and realised that although he had not deliberately drawn a picture since high school art class, he had been drawing these feathers for years: while talking on the phone, sitting at meetings or when waiting for people. They were definitely part of him.

He began to wonder what other symbols or objects reflected who he really was, and as he waited for his friend he began to add other doodles to the back of his notebook. To his surprise many of the things he added were shapes and images he associated with the Native American culture.

Although Brad is one-eighth Cherokee on his grandfather's side, he had not realised how significant this aspect of his heritage was until he drew his Coat of Arms. Brad found that exploring his Cherokee background further, through books and interviewing tribal Elders, was a meaningful path to his Authentic Self.

An Animal Symbol

If you could be any animal, what would you choose to be? Chances are your choice says something about your Authentic Self. Draw a picture of this animal, and then write a description of the animal's special characteristics and habits. What qualities do you find most appealing about this animal?

Now imagine that you are in fact the animal you have selected, and take some time to imagine yourself as this animal. How would you spend a typical day? What do you like and dislike about being this animal?

Louise named a rabbit as her favourite animal, imagining a large light brown jack-rabbit that she had seen in her childhood when she was growing up in a small Arizona desert town.

She described the rabbit as quiet and shy. In thinking about rabbits she realised they are resourceful because "You have to be when you are that small and vulnerable". In imagining a typical day in the life of a rabbit, she noted that rabbits burrow in the earth and that they are vegetarian. If necessary they will use their sharp claws to defend themselves and their babies. A rabbit knows how to take care of itself.

In identifying with the rabbit, Louise realised some valuable things about herself: that she was resourceful, she could take care of herself, and though shy, she was capable of defending or protecting herself.

After doing this exercise, Louise found it meaningful to place an image of a rabbit on her desk as a way to further connect and identify with her Authentic Self. What object or picture would help you identify with the animal you chose for this exercise?

A Tree that Speaks to You
This exercise needs to be done when you have time to walk around outdoors in a wooded setting. The tree is a device upon which you can project your thoughts, feelings and special awareness, thereby allowing your Authentic Self to speak to you.

 One Small Step
Give yourself at least an hour to walk around and contemplate various trees. Look for a tree that you find particularly appealing. Imagine that this tree has something to tell you about your Authentic Self. Imagine that the tree knows something important about you because you are kindred spirits. Ask the tree to tell you how you are alike, and write down what comes to mind. Then ask the tree to tell you the message it has for you about your Authentic Self, and write down whatever you imagine the tree tells you.

Here is the response that came to me while contemplating a tall ponderosa pine in a mountain meadow:

> You and I are alike because we have stood in the same place for a long while, enduring snow and rain and drought. Because we endured we know we can survive the winter to come and the hot summer days that will follow again next year. On a typical day I watch the sunrise, listen to the bird songs, feel the wind against my branches and take special joy in seeing the sunset give way to a sky full of stars. The special message I have for you is to notice the big

blue sky above you and the beautiful clouds, the wild flowers, squirrels and hummingbirds beneath it. Enjoying what is here with you right now is important. You spend too much time worrying and not enough time allowing yourself to enjoy the moment.

This exercise can be repeated on various walks in the future, choosing whatever tree appeals to you on each walk.

Totem Doll

Historically, doll-making is practiced to develop nurturing and maturity. Young girls in Africa once made fertility dolls for themselves as a preparation for puberty, marriage and childbearing. In many different traditions, dolls have been made for spiritual purposes.

Inspired in part by African tribal dolls, and borrowing ideas from Native American totem poles and European coats of arms, I began experimenting with what has evolved into Totem Dolls. A Totem Doll can be whatever size you wish. You can attach to it whatever articles you feel symbolise who you are.

A Totem Doll can be used to represent who you were, who you are and who you wish to become. One doll can represent the various aspects of your life; or, if you prefer, you can make different dolls for the past, the present and the future.

Susan, who had suffered a painful knee operation, included a gash of red fabric across the knee of her doll. Since she had grown up near the woods and had loved the forest as a child, she also included a piece of pine bark in the doll's stuffing.

She then added things to symbolise her current self. These included a wedding band sewn onto the doll's hand, a miniature book with the names of her three children written inside it, and a small bag labelled "manure" that symbolised some of the political corruption she was dealing with in her work at a major corporation. (The bag did not contain real manure for obvious aesthetic and olfactory reasons!).

To represent her future self, Susan drew some attractive wrinkles on the doll's face. She added some strands of white to the pieces of brown string she had used to depict her hair. She added another bag, attached to the doll's waist, and labeled it "Free Time". On a small piece of paper rolled up like a scroll, she wrote MBA, symbolising her achievement of the graduate degree she was pursuing.

Susan is twenty years younger than her husband, and she fears he will die before her. To reflect her future grief over his death, she tied a small piece of black fabric around the doll's upper arm. The fabric was torn, not cut, so that the raw edges would reflect the raw feelings she anticipates. On top of the miniature book with her children's names, she tied a second book. Inside this one she wrote "Memories of good times with Jim", which she knows will comfort her at some time in the future.

Maggie responded to the Totem Doll exercise by first making a small doll that represented herself as a child. Marks on the doll's head depicted the emotional abuse she had endured, and marks on its body to symbolise other kinds of abuse.

A piece of wavy blue paper depicted the ocean she had loved as a child, and a yellow bead represented the sun. Seashells worked naturally as articles of clothing for this doll; as a little girl she had fantasised that she was a mermaid.

To symbolise the present, Maggie made a larger doll to remind herself she is older, bigger and less vulnerable than the "mermaid child." She cut out words from magazines and pasted them directly onto the doll to describe various virtues and faults she saw as being true of her present self.

She also added articles to reflect activities she enjoys - a sprig of dried herb to reflect her love of cooking, a piece of an old shoelace to remember her daily jogging. It was not until she was drawing a mouth onto her Present Doll that she realised that her smaller, younger doll had no mouth. As a child she had been mute in her pain. She went back and drew a mouth on the Past Doll to represent her healing and growth.

It was several weeks before Maggie felt ready to make a doll representing the future. She decided to make it out of the same cloth as the other two dolls, since it represented a continuation of the self. But she wanted this doll to look older, as Maggie would be in the future. She dipped the remaining fabric in strong brewed tea to make it look more aged. She then glued two stars for eyes to depict the wisdom of age.

Tickled by the idea that she would allow herself to be more expressive and even eccentric when she was old, she visited toy stores and looked at commercial dolls' clothes until she found a hat that she could decorate with a bright red rose and a small paper butterfly. Maggie does not consider her Future Doll completed, and may well add things to it for many years to come. I asked her, "What will you do if the Future Doll becomes too small for all the things you want to add to it?"

She smiled and answered, "Then I will make a bigger Future Doll, and before I stuff it, I will put this doll inside it, so it is an integral part of the new doll. Maybe I'll fasten some of the things from this doll onto the bigger one, or maybe I'll just leave them inside. What is important is I that know they are in there."

 One Small Step
Sew a doll by machine or by hand and decorate it with buttons, beads, paper or whatever objects represent you. Books with

instructions for making small and large dolls are readily obtained
from craft shops or libraries. These instructions can be adapted to
make your own self-expressive doll.

Don't be intimidated by the idea of making a Totem Doll to represent
yourself. On the wall of the room where I do most of my creative work, I
have tacked a small sign which says, "Show me a person who never made
a mistake, and I'll show you person who never made anything!"

Loose stitches and less-than-perfect craftsmanship only add to the
charm and evocative personality of a home made Totem Doll that
represents your Authentic Self.

As an alternative to sewing a doll, you can contact a doll-maker and
commission a doll that represents an aspect of your inner self. Look at
examples of the doll-maker's work to ensure that the doll reflects a style
that fits you. Ask the doll-maker to draw a model of the doll before
constructing it to ensure that the resulting doll is what you had in mind.

Even easier and less costly is making a paper Totem Doll. In *Reclaiming
Herstory*, Cheryl Bell-Gadsby and Ann Siegenberg suggest decorating
paper dolls to symbolise yourself. The paper dolls can be decorated in the
same manner as the fabric Totem Dolls. The only disadvantage is that they
are more fragile, and some people find they are not as personally evocative
as the three-dimensional dolls.

Other Creative Paths to the Authentic Self

Dancing; writing poetry, stories, or plays; painting or drawing; quilting or
singing - the creative paths to the Authentic Self are endless. The best
guide is what appeals to you. If you long for further exploration but are
not sure what you want to do, try several weekly "artist's dates" to inspire
your creative side. You might take a class, visit museums, exhibitions, art
supply stores or simply experiment with following your own whims. Do
not be daunted by the "critic within". Most creative people proceed
despite an inner critic.

In *The Artist's Way*, Julia Cameron suggests making a weekly "artist's
date" with yourself. The artist's date consists of setting aside at least an
hour and a half to pursue activities you would not normally get to
experience; it is simply time to explore the creative aspect of your
Authentic Self.

Especially when practiced on a regular basis, the artist's date can be a
powerful and rewarding way to foster a connection with that aspect of
your Authentic Self that is the source of all your creative pursuits.

CONNECTING TO YOUR AUTHENTIC SELF THROUGH RELAXATION AND PLAY

There are many ways to reconnect with and explore your Authentic Self. Some of the most powerful techniques are often the most enjoyable.

Taking Time to Just Be

Perhaps you already give yourself permission to spend a few minutes each day just letting yourself "be". If so, you are a rare person, as many of us in Western society live frenetic lives. The gift of fifteen or twenty minutes a day of unstructured time in which you quietly rest, contemplate, or allow your mind to wander is a rewarding way to connect to your Authentic Self. An enjoyable way to approach this time is to notice where in your body you feel most comfortable and to allow that comfort to spread to the rest of your body.

Taking a Mini-Vacation

It took me a long time to recognise the difference between being exhausted and being lazy or depressed. Many times in the past I would find myself without energy. Inevitably, I would accuse myself of being lazy or diagnose myself as depressed. The antidote for these things, I had been taught, was structure and activity. And so I would make a list of productive things to do that day, and proceed to do them as efficiently as possible.

The next day, like clockwork, I would become ill. Usually it was characterised by a fever and flu symptoms that kept me in bed for a day or more. More recently, I have learned to take time off to rest when I begin to experience the state I once labelled as laziness or depression.

Last week I had just such a day. Once the essential things were done (bathing, brushing my teeth, feeding my pets, returning a few phone calls), I allowed myself to take a mini-vacation. I began by drinking tea by the fireplace. I listened to good music, embroidered the face on a rag doll, napped, caught up on some reading, telephoned several friends and ended with a long, luxurious bubble bath. After a few hours, I emerged refreshed and energised. The next day I felt fine.

If you already spend a lot of unstructured time, taking time off may be redundant and not particularly useful. In this case, activity may be a better means to self-renewal. However, if you tend to be very active and are now feeling stale or tired, you may benefit from a taking a few hours off in which you just let yourself "be". Furthermore, it may prevent you from becoming ill.

One Small Step
If you were to take a mini-vacation, would it be characterised by rest and quiet relaxation like mine, or would it be more active and involve leaving your accustomed environment for a few hours?

Focusing Your Attention

Focusing your attention on the present is a natural way to connect with and more vividly experience your Authentic Self. As children, we are born with this ability, but unfortunately most of us are robbed of it during the journey to adulthood.

Yesterday afternoon in the supermarket, I saw a small girl holding a mango in her hand as she sat quietly in her mother's grocery cart. She was oblivious of her surroundings, and her face held an expression of rapt attention. With the wonderful lack of self-consciousness inherent in young children, her fingers prodded, squeezed and stroked the rosy surface of the mango, as if she was trying to learn all of the secrets of "mango-ness".

Preoccupied with phone calls I needed to return and letters I had to write, I had been hurrying through the supermarket intent on finishing the job of grocery-shopping as quickly as possible. Seeing that wonderful little girl stopped me in my tracks. She was at that moment happily living in the "estate" of her Authentic Self. Clearly I was not.

I had been traversing the market at record speed but proceeding on automatic pilot, my mind elsewhere. I had not even registered the symphony of jewel-like shapes and colours in the well-stocked summer produce. I had missed out on the exquisite sunset shades of the ripening peaches, the wine-coloured raspberries, the crimson cherries, all their scents mingling agreeably with the soothing aroma of fresh-baked bread. After seeing that little girl, I resolved to slow down and focus on the moment.

 One Small Step
Take a moment now to notice the shapes, colours, smells and textures around you. Focus on what you re experiencing as you do so.

An Ericksonian Relaxation Method

The Ericksonian Relaxation Method (Dolan, 1991) helps you to reclaim your natural ability to enjoy the moment that painful or traumatic experiences disrupt. It is also a good way to nurture yourself during or after a hectic day, and can be used to encourage sleep at night.

This is a very powerful technique, so please read all the instructions before proceeding with the exercise. Under no circumstances should this exercise be done while driving a car or using machinery.

One Small Step

Find a comfortable position in which your body feels well supported. Focus your gaze on some pleasant or restful view. Nature is often a preferred choice, however some people enjoy looking at an uncluttered wall. If you find yourself in a jarring or tense environment, you might prefer simply to gaze at a pretty postcard, or some other object that you like. It doesn't matter what you choose to look at, as long as it is not disturbing.

Concentrating only on what you are viewing, name five things that you see. Now name five things that you hear, and five physical sensations.

(Don't worry if you can't think of five different things for each category. It's fine to repeat the same thing; for example, "I see a tree. I still see a tree." Everything you name is to be something that you see in front of you from your present position.)

Once you have completed five for each category, name four for each category, that is: four sights, four sounds, four physical sensations. Continue by naming three for each category, two for each category, and one for each category.

When you reach one, you can either continue the process by starting again at five, or you can simply stop and enjoy the sensation of vividly experiencing the moment. If you get confused or lose your place before you reach one, simply stop and enjoy the experience of deep relaxation and communion with your Authentic Self.

If you are very tired when you are doing this technique, you may fall asleep. In fact, it can be used as a way to relax into sleep by repeating it until you drift off. If you are doing this to get to sleep in a darkened room with little to see, you may want to simply repeat, "I see the darkened space in front of me" for the visual category. As an alternative, if you prefer to keep your eyes closed, you could choose to skip the sights category.

When using this method, feel free to stop at any time as you progress from five to one, and simply enjoy the experience of fully connecting to what you see, hear and feel in the present moment.

For some hypnotically gifted individuals, doing this exercise will result in a light hypnotic trance. This is an example of the "common everyday trance" that occurs naturally when people become pleasantly absorbed in an everyday experience, such as watching a good film, looking at a beautiful sunset or, like the little girl, enjoying a mango in the supermarket.

If at any time during or after the exercise you want to become more focused and alert, the easiest way to shift away from the wide attention is to physically move. Stand up and walk around the room. If you are feeling sleepy or spacey and wish to shift back to a more alert state, count yourself back into alertness: 1) I am more and more alert and refreshed, 2) I am even more alert, 3) I am even more refreshed and alert, 4) I am even more refreshed, 5) I am fully alert and refreshed.

After doing this relaxation exercise, take some time to rest and connect with your Authentic Self.

This chapter has offered a wide range of possibilities to help you reclaim and further enjoy the "estate" of your Authentic Self. Return to the sections that nurture and replenish you. The next chapter will invite you to continue and further develop this process of "coming home" to your Authentic Self by exploring ways to enhance your quality of everyday life in your home environment.

CHAPTER TWO
WELCOME HOME!

If there is harmony in the house
There will be order in the nation.
If there is order in the nation
There will be peace in the world.

– Chinese Proverb

After a good dinner, one can forgive anybody,
even one's own relatives.

– Oscar Wilde

As a reflection of the people who live there, home is a natural symbol for the self and your beliefs about how life should be lived. Spending time at home engaged in simple and cozy activities has recently become a national trend in America, as evidenced by the popularity of magazines devoted to cooking, crafts, decorating and other homey pursuits. Divided into four sections, this chapter introduces suggestions to increase your delight in your home.

GREETING EVERYDAY GIFTS

This chapter invites you to explore various ways to enhance the quality of your everyday life at home. When first exploring these ideas, some people, particularly those who have suffered childhood abuse or neglect, find themselves questioning whether they deserve good things in their home life on a daily basis. When asked to envision how she could enhance the quality of her everyday life, Connie, a business manager at a busy medical office, had the following response:

Working on creating a home that pleases me, establishing daily rituals just to make myself feel good, are ideas that would have been considered trivial or even selfish in the family where I grew up. I mean, it's like giving myself a gift everyday for no reason at all. Do I really deserve this?

A month later Connie had a different perspective:

After the first few weeks of doing these things I realised that my self-nurturing at home was having a ripple effect. Because my own needs were being met, I was more patient and tolerant with my family and other people both at home and at work. My relationships were improving.

Regardless of whether being good to yourself was encouraged in your childhood, and perhaps even more so if it was not, you have a right to experience life-affirming personal rituals and a pleasant place to live. Keep in mind that nurturing will *increase*, rather than decrease, your ability to nurture others.

Nurturing Daily Rituals

When I was a young girl there was a part of the weekday that never varied. I would come home from school at four o'clock, and my mother would be sitting at the table drinking a cup of tea. Usually there would be a friend visiting, but even if she was alone, she would stop and give herself that time of respite before starting dinner.

Often I would join her. The little room where she always took her tea looked out on an old pear tree, and this marked the seasons of our tea drinking. I remember her laughing one Autumn afternoon as she watched our fat old cat leaping around under that pear tree, trying to catch each leaf as it dropped to the ground.

The pear tree's branches became bare against the grey winter sky; in Spring came the pale blossoms; and in Summer the promise of the birds who would eat the pears that fell to the ground. My mother's tea drinking was a small and ordinary daily ceremony, yet it added a reassuring continuity to my life, and I suspect to hers also. Our family moved many times over the years and the tea drinking may have eased the transitions by providing a reassuring constancy in the daily patterns of our household.

These days, like my mother, I stop whatever I am doing at four o'clock. But it is for a different ceremony. I stand at the edge of the garden and listen. After a moment I hear the hoof-beats of the wild elk running down the valley on their way to the pond. Soon I see them approaching and watch entranced as they leap playfully over the wildflowers and pine seedlings, and then pass out of sight over the hill. It seems that they also have predictable daily patterns.

In our modern world with its frantic pace, simple rituals that bestow comfort have become increasingly important. While such rituals naturally vary from person to person, they share the common purpose of humanising and enriching one's daily life.

I enjoy observing the rituals of daily life around me. My friend Linda does yoga every morning. David begins his day with a cup of fragrant tea. Paula takes stock of what her garden needs before she leaves for work, and all day looks forward to working in the soil that evening. Gardening helps her deal with the ups and downs of everyday life. She says her grandmother was the same way, and would take out her garden hoe whenever she was upset about something, working things out in her mind as she worked the earth.

Mark and Julie take a walk together in the foothills every morning before going to work. Taking to work flowers from his garden brings Michael a sense of peacefulness at his job. Charlie takes a few minutes during his working day to play solitaire on his computer. He emerges refreshed and relaxed and continues his work tasks with renewed creativity.

Steve takes a nightly walk just before going to bed. Luke listens to classical music on Sunday morning while ironing his shirts for the week. Insoo finds it calming and centring to clean her house. Several people told me that cleaning and re-organising closets and drawers relaxes them, providing something to do while mentally exploring and clarifying thoughts and creative ideas.

Most mornings, before reading the newspaper or speaking to anyone, my husband goes outdoors and feeds the wild birds who congregate outside our kitchen window. He then spends a few minutes quietly sipping his coffee while listening to their songs and conversations.

Marilyn spends an hour each night doing needlepoint while she watches the evening news. The rhythmic stitching reminds her to slow down and enjoy the moments of her life. When her three children were teenagers, the needlepoint helped her cope with the stress of bringing up adolescents and gave her a much-needed respite of peace and quiet as she waited up for them at night. Although her children have now grown into responsible adults, Marilyn still benefits from her evening needlepoint ritual. With each stitch her breathing becomes more calm and even. After an hour her hands and eyes are tired and her mind is relaxed.

A busy accountant with a high-pressured schedule, Michael runs every morning wherever he is, regardless of the weather. While most people exercise to benefit their body, Michael does it to enhance his mental functioning later in the day. He says that running early in the morning clears the cobwebs from his mind, and he feels more alert all day.

For several years Debra and her women friends have shared the magic of a monthly walk in the mountain forest under the full moon. They have done this in soft spring rain, blowing snow, on tranquil summer nights, and in every other imaginable kind of weather. The effect is always one of wonder at the beauty of nature, and a renewed appreciation of the friendship they share.

Angela burns a stick of delicately perfumed sandalwood incense every night just before she goes to bed, careful to keep it contained in a safe holder. She loves the experience of drifting off to sleep while inhaling the exquisite fragrance and awakening to its subtle scent still lingering throughout the house.

Louise, a busy mother of seven school-age children, tells me she makes time to quilt a little each evening. She is often too tired to relax completely enough to just sit quietly in the evening and rest, even though she knows that would be good for her. But the needle and thread in her hand allow her to make the transition from intense busyness to a sense of tranquility.

Kerry picks up a novel at night for the same reason that Louise quilts. Many people describe nightly reading as an important part of their lives. Several explained that when stressed they found "trying" to relax in order to fall asleep generally increased their restlessness, but reading for a few minutes provided an effortless transition into a restful state.

What they choose to read before sleep varied, but since the content of what we hear or see just before falling asleep is likely to show up in our dreams, it is worthwhile to consciously select the books we read or the TV shows we watch late at night.

Carla stretches each night for several minutes before going to bed. She says these movements simultaneously calm her mind and relax her body. Before she started stretching she used to wake in the morning with stiff muscles. Now she gets out of bed with ease, ready to greet the day.

Writing is an important ritual for me. I have kept a journal for more than twenty years. If more than a few days pass without taking time for the journal, I become restless and irritable. I have written on crowded buses and trains, while riding in a dugout canoe on a swampy river in a Central American rainforest, inside primitive thatched huts and in elegant European tea-rooms. The effect is always the same: a renewed sense of contact with my inner self, an appreciation for the world around me and an accompanying peacefulness.

Possibilities

What are your nurturing daily rituals?

What daily ceremonies have you observed in others that appeal to you?

Do you want to incorporate any of these into your own life? If so, choose one that is especially appealing or create one of your own and experiment with it this week.

The Comfort of Food

Food can be a comforting experience as well as a ritual of celebration. Despite the advent of trends towards low-fat cooking, fast-food and take-out food and the increased sophistication created by the availability of ethnically varied global cuisine, people continue to crave the simple foods of their childhood, sometimes referred to as "comfort food".

Holly remembers a difficult time at age ten when her mother was hospitalised for cancer and for several days wavered near death. A housekeeper, Mrs Robinson was hired to manage the house, cook and care for Holly and her two younger sisters. Almost immediately she began preparing the children's favourite foods, the same ones their mother usually cooked. This brought a much-needed sense of comfort and reassurance. Years later Holly asked Mrs Robinson how she knew what their favourite foods were.

Mrs Robinson smiled, "That was easy. I just opened your mother's cookbook and found the pages that had food stains. The more food stains, the more I figured you liked the recipe."

Last year, while teaching a seminar in Belgium, I stayed at the home of a colleague who lives in the small village that was the ancestral home of my great-grandmother. Tired at the end of the day, I decided to take a nap before dinner. I awakened with a pervasive feeling of well-being.

I soon identified the source of my good feelings. The fragrances wafting from the kitchen up to my room were familiar ones, the same ones I had smelled many times in my grandmother's kitchen. My host, a gifted cook, had prepared a local Belgian dish. The same recipe must have travelled across the ocean with great grandmother Flavia and been faithfully passed on to her daughter.

What foods do you associate with comfort and well-being? Are these part of your current life? If not, might they be a source of comfort or reassurance during stressful times?

When I interviewed people about what they associated with rituals of celebration, many described special foods, cloth napkins and candles on the table. Some people mentioned costly foods and beverages: champagne, caviar, lobster. But not all food associated with festive occasions is costly.

For Kathleen, it wouldn't be Thanksgiving without her mother's chestnut stuffing. Keith notes wryly that he while he hates the Midwestern American tradition of "suspending canned fruits in bowls of surrealistically coloured gelatin", it wouldn't be Christmas without his grandmother's canned apricot-studded lime-jelly trifle. And so he makes one every year, much to the amusement and mock horror of his partner.

You can start your own new traditions. As a teenager, because I loved the fragrance and taste of gingerbread, I began to bake gingerbread men at Christmas for the rest of my family. I have now been baking gingerbread every winter for thirty years. Although this was not a tradition passed down to me by any relative, it has become a meaningful one for me.

Other foods that were not part of my childhood but which have become personal traditions over the past fifteen years are a spicy Southwestern Chocolate Bread Pudding and a New Orleans Chicken Andouille Gumbo. I serve these at various festive family gatherings, and friends have been known to phone ahead to make sure I am including them on the menu! For me, "family" means close friends as well as relatives.

Though starting new traditions may seem a little odd at first, there can be many advantages: healthier or more colourful and appealing food that you introduce as a new tradition can become a positive legacy to your descendants.

If your family of origin tended to act out pain, violence or other forms of dysfunction during holiday gatherings, the traditional foods you associate with those occasions may induce sadness. In this case, introducing new foods or different food preparations to your own celebrations can be especially valuable. Preparing and serving food that is special but different to what your family ate can help you move beyond painful past memories to establish new and positive mental associations with future holidays. And as you prepare and serve your own special foods on holidays over the course of several years, these dishes will take on a meaningful aura of ritual and tradition.

If you would like to establish new food traditions for your own holidays and special occasions and want further ideas, cookbooks from various countries can be an interesting resource. Traditional ethnic cooking is based on culinary wisdom that evolved according to the availability of various ingredients in the locale where it developed. Contemporary cookbooks that feature light and healthy food can also be a useful source of new ideas. Select from various customs as you create and evolve your own traditions.

Possibilities
Which foods do you most associate with festive occasions?

Are there new foods you would enjoy introducing into future holidays or other seasonal special celebrations?

Would you enjoy exploring new ideas from cookbooks or friends' recipe files?

What might be the first step to creating a new tradition of your own for a festive occasion?

SURROUNDING YOURSELF WITH WHAT YOU LOVE

Your home is your private sanctuary and should be aesthetically pleasing as well as functional. Decorate your walls and floors with your favourite colours and textures; display your favourite objects; create your own sense of beauty.

Painting Walls and More
What colours lift your spirits? Do you love warm or cool colours? Do you find pastels soothing? Are you invigorated and refreshed by bright, intense saturated colours? Or do you prefer the serenity of a monochromatic colour scheme warmed by touches of wood? Or perhaps you prefer the restful tones of neutral colours such as white, black, grey or tan.

Since childhood, I have been crazy about the combination of bright blue and yellow. Just before I began to write this, I was out in my backyard garden cutting stems of intense yellow moonglow yarrow and placing them in small cobalt blue glass jars and bottles that I have collected over many years.

Unfortunately a population of tiny insects love the moonglow yarrow as much as I do, so I have to wash each flower individually before bringing them into the house. It's a laborious process, but worth it because of the delight I feel every time I walk into the kitchen and feast my eyes on the thirty little blue and yellow bouquets that line the window sills. Why do I go to all this trouble? Simply because it makes me happy.

There are many ways to introduce the colours you love into your home. Althea collects pieces of beautiful fabrics in her favourite colours and drapes them around her house to delight her eyes. She explains, "This is how I store fabrics!" Eventually Althea makes some of the fabrics into garments or linens. Others she leaves attractively draped for years, or gives them away to friends, relatives or Oxfam. She has hung curtain rods not only across windows but throughout her house, and enjoys draping fabrics on these for variety and pleasure, as well as for the privacy they provide.

Walking along the Pacific ocean near her home, Samantha literally stumbled on a piece of beautiful green glass. It was her favourite shade of green. Its once jagged edges had been rounded and polished by the sand and water. She fell in love with the soft green tones of the glass and began to look for additional pieces during her daily walks on the beach. Her house is now decorated with many pieces of beautiful polished green glass, all gifts from the sea.

Joanna enjoys many different colours. In the Spring and Summer she is drawn to restful pastels. When the leaves begin to turn in the New England village where she lives, she craves russets, golds and browns, and in the Winter she says with her typical enthusiasm, "I just can't get enough red!"

Although she is not a wealthy woman, Joanna has found a way to satisfy her large and varied appetite for colour. The interior of her small house is neutral with white walls. Her few pieces of furniture are covered with washable cream-coloured slipcovers. However, the covers on the cushions that adorn the furniture and the cloth that covers her kitchen table change with the seasons.

Paint is a time-honored way to add colour to a home. A decorator observed that in proportion to the effects achieved, a can of paint may be one of the best bargains for introducing change into your living environment. Moreover, some paint and DIY stores sell unclaimed, rejected or left over custom-mixed paints at extremely discounted prices. But paint doesn't need to be limited to walls.

My friend Richard loves purple. One day he took a paintbrush and playfully painted small details in a beautiful shade of purple in unexpected places throughout his living space. Then he walked outdoors and added touches to the outside of his house and to his garage.

One of the last touches he added was the word, "Yes!" written in purple paint. Whenever I visit his home, this expression of purple exuberance delights me. I imagine it delights Richard and his wife and daughter on a daily basis.

My sister Laura especially loves vibrantly coloured painted surfaces on furniture as well as walls. The mother of a mischievous, very active young son, she knew that the fragile painted surfaces of the furniture she admired in galleries would not stand up to the wear and tear of his playtime. So she literally took matters into her own hands. Wanting to experiment with paint effects and designs, she began collecting old wooden chairs, tables and cabinets so decrepit looking that no one else wanted them.

As her painting and designing skills developed, she redecorated some of her earliest pieces with fresh paint. She now lives in the colourfully painted folk art environment she once coveted, and no longer worries about the potential effects of her child's antics on the furniture since she can always touch it up!

Bringing Nature Indoors

Do you like being surrounded by living things? Perhaps you find the constantly moving shapes of colourful fish in an aquarium especially relaxing. Or maybe you prefer the four-footed affection of a faithful dog or cat. As my friend Diane once observed, "Cats are ever-changing, living, soft sculpture." Actually, this is true of all living things.

Do plants comfort you in your living space? If you especially love the forest, perhaps you would enjoy having a living tree in your home. Or, if you love the desert, a cactus could simulate the open spaces that soothe your soul. Green plants and trees help purify the air, while providing a calming leafy backdrop for all your everyday activities.

A couple I know live in the Rocky Mountains, but also love the ocean. Their bathroom shelves are filled with large and small seashells they have collected from beaches during various vacations. These things cost nothing but time, yet provide reminders of treasured vacations. Another similarly minded person has hanging in her office a picture of herself swimming with dolphins.

 Possibilities
What appeals to you from the outdoors?
How might you evoke this in your home?

Delighting in Textures

Eighteen-month-old Daniel squeals with delight when his toes touch velvet. Sammy, my cat, loves freshly laundered cotton. The moment he curls up on a quilt he signals his pleasure with loud purring. Texture is an often overlooked source of pleasure and comfort.

 Possibilities
Do you prefer smooth or rough textures?
If you had your choice, would you select leather, wood, velvet, linen, cotton or silk for a favourite chair?
What sort of textures feel best to you?

Inside his home, the Chilean poet, Pablo Neruda, paved a hallway in

small rounded stones specifically so he could enjoy the cobbled surface
with his bare feet. In the outdoor primitive courtyard off our living-room, I
planted woolly thyme for the same reason Neruda arranged his stones for
the pleasure it gives bare feet.

On a recent visit, my mother exclaimed over the softness of the much-
washed cotton sheets I had used to make her bed. They reminded her of
the long-ago feeling of her girlhood bed.

Sarah covered all her chairs with a patchwork of old linen fabrics,
chosen less for colour than for their cool feel during the hot, humid
summers where she lives.

Alan collects baskets, especially favouring old ones in various stages of
disrepair. He loves the look and feel of their worn surfaces, displaying
them carefully on the wall where they can be touched as well as seen.

Mary chooses pottery cups and dishes specifically for their feel,
preferring the look and heft of oddly shaped oversized pieces. Betsy
swears her tea tastes better when she wraps her fingers around a thin
porcelain cup.

The potential for enjoying texture at home is as unlimited as your
imagination. Let your hands, eyes and creativity guide you as you take
some time now to imagine how you might incorporate into your home the
textures that delight you.

Art in Your Home
My husband and I bought art before we bought furniture, preferring to
feast our eyes instead of cushioning our bodies. Even so, our taste often
outstripped our budget. By necessity we learned to settle at times for
signed posters and lithographs instead of original pieces by the artists we
loved. Sometimes, mass-produced reproductions were the only way we
could afford to introduce a particular artist's vision into our environment.

When as a young woman struggling to make ends meet even posters
were out of reach, I did what my grandmother and mother had done
before me and looked for beauty wherever I could find it. Fortunately I
didn't have to look far. Thanks to an extended family that always included
small children, I have never been without their gifts of colourful and
creative original finger-paintings, drawings and clay sculptures. Each one
was a treasure conveying a unique and personal childhood world. As
Picasso once said, "It takes a long time to see like a child."

But perhaps you like "grown-up" art as well. If you are not yet sure
what style of art most appeals to you, begin by visiting galleries and
museums. A fun game to play with children and adults when visiting
museums and galleries is to pretend that you will each be allowed to take
home one piece of art. Deciding which piece you would choose when you
visit an exhibition will help you explore and define your own taste in art.

Try to imagine yourself living with the piece over many years. How would it look in various rooms in your house? Never buy art under pressure, especially if it entails a sizeable financial investment. If necessary, walk out of the gallery so that you can contemplate your decision without the pressure of a salesperson.

If you love art but your current budget is tight, don't despair. You can often purchase a piece over time, or perhaps arrange with the artist to trade one of your skills in exchange for artwork. If you live near a college or university, watch for the Art Department's yearly sales of works by talented students.

Nick loves good art, and rejoiced when he finally moved into a spare uncluttered house with lots of empty wall space for the framed original paintings he had always coveted. Unfortunately the style and quality of artwork Nick loves are currently beyond his budget. He was depressed at the thought of coming home to bare walls every night for the next several years while saving for one really good piece.

As an interim solution, Nick decided to use the postcard prints he had been collecting for years from visits to numerous art museums. Individually matted and set in elegant second-hand frames that he had refinished, the postcards displayed some of the world's best art, and reminded Nick of his favourite museums.

 One Small Step
The first small step is discovering what you love. Have you already begun?

ARRANGING AND REARRANGING YOUR HOME

The arrangement of furniture and other objects in your home should reflect and support your lifestyle. They should be functional but also attractive. But most of all, your home environment should nourish and revitalise your spirit.

The Ascetics of Order

As a young child I was influenced by my maternal grandmother's opinions on the ascetics of cleanliness and order. One day as she energetically scoured her kitchen sink, she told me: "Vonnie, filth can transform a beautiful house into a trash heap, and cleanliness can bring a feeling of peacefulness and beauty to the most humble shack. Don't forget this."

Her manner indicated that she had shared an important secret, probably one she had learned from her own grandmother or her mother. She viewed cleaning her house as a way not only of restoring but also of creating peace and beauty. After hearing these ideas, I began making my bed first thing in the morning and keeping my bedroom in good order, habits which continue to this day. Although I didn't realise it until years later, grandma opened my eyes to the action of cleaning or tidying as a magical, alchemical activity that transforms an environment.

The functionality of cleanliness and order, the convenience of being easily able to find one's belongings and having them in good repair, allows us to move gracefully through the day, freeing up time to spend on achieving a rewarding life.

If taken too far, however, the ascetic of order and cleanliness causes its own problems. When taken to an extreme and unrealistic level, the quest for a clean and orderly home can become a form of enslavement. In such cases, it interferes with rather than enhances the living of a rewarding life, leaving no time for creative and meaningful pursuits.

Not surprisingly, the optimal level of order and cleanliness needed for living well varies from person to person. Artists and musicians know the importance of having their tools and instruments ready at hand when the muse strikes, even if this results in cluttering their living space.

Given the reality of your current living situation, what do you like about the way you have organised your living space? Are there things you could change at home that might enhance your daily life?

Your response to the above questions may not necessarily be about organisation. It may have more to do with improving the quality of everyday life in other ways, as it was for Ron.

Ron complained:

> I spend several minutes every morning looking for matching socks, belts and shirts in my closet. I wake up wanting a cup of coffee and I get so frustrated when ten minutes pass and I'm still in the closet trying to get dressed! It puts me in a foul mood every morning.

Asked what would be the first and smallest sign that things were getting better, he answered:

> I'd give myself a cup of coffee first thing in the morning and take it back into the closet with me. It would be a lot less frustrating if I was drinking that first cup of coffee while I was searching for clothes. I need to put a little shelf up in the corner of my closet so I have a place to set that coffee cup while I'm pulling out things to wear.

When asked about further signs that his morning ritual was getting better or more enjoyable, he answered:

> I would be listening to good music on the radio while I was looking for my stuff in the morning.

These details could make a difference in the quality of Ron's living space, but at no point was he interested in cleaning or re-organising his closet! It didn't fit for him, and it was not something he would do.

 Possibilities
What do you like about the way that you approach each day in your living space?
Are there things that you would like to change in some way? If so, what would be the result of that difference?
What would be the one small step towards making that change?

Designing with Furniture

Don't be afraid to be unconventional in arranging your home. One Winter, my sister Lisa moved her living room couch into the kitchen because it was the coziest place in the house. Eccentric furniture arrangements and unusual touches are a form of joyous self-expression that can reinvent a living environment while enlivening its inhabitants.

 Possibilities
Do you prefer to sit on chairs, couches or pillows?
When choosing furniture, do dramatic or primitive shapes appeal to you, or do you prefer more traditional designs?
Perhaps you enjoy the detail of ornate wood carvings, or maybe the opposite. Perhaps you like the streamlined effect of clean, modern decor?
Or do you like an absence of furniture, preferring a few large pillows or a luxurious rug to couches and chairs?

The Ancient Perspective of Feng Shui

When exploring new ideas for arranging your home and furniture you might enjoy incorporating Feng Shui teachings. An ancient Chinese philosophy about the relationships between humans and their environment, Feng Shui was developed over five thousand years ago. The purpose of this art is to improve the quality of life by creating environments that are in harmony with nature.

Practitioners of Feng Shui (pronounced "phong shway") believe that modifications in layout and orientation of homes and work-places can enhance the well being of the people who inhabit those spaces. Increasingly popular in the West, books on Feng Shui are readily available in most bookstores and libraries. *The Complete Illustrated Guide to Feng Shui: How to Apply the Secrets of Chinese Wisdom for Health, Wealth and Happiness* by Lillian Too is a good introduction.

CHALLENGING THE PROSPERITY MIND-SET

What do you associate with prosperity? I ask this question because people often tell me wistfully that life in their home would be much better if only they were "rich", or if only they had more money. My sister, a counsellor, likes to ask people how their lives would be different if they won the Lottery.

While some people respond to the Lottery question with descriptions of things that only additional money could buy, most people also list things that are not dependent on acquiring additional money. Once identified, at least some of the things you associate with prosperity may be well within reach.

Possibilities
What are the things you associate with a pleasing, prosperous life?
What aspects of these things are more associated with behaviour or personal style than money?
Which are more dependent on money?
Can you give some of these things to yourself now?
How might you use your personal creativity to facilitate this?
What would be the first small step?

Roger told me that the things he associated with "living the good life" included driving an expensive sports car, fresh flowers on the dining room table, real butter in the refrigerator and drinking a glass of wine with dinner. While he could not afford the expensive sports car, with a little planning he could grow the flowers in the garden outside his kitchen door, keep a small package of butter in the refrigerator, and enjoy a glass of wine with dinner.

Tanya associates prosperity with velvety textures, dark carved woods, and silver candlesticks, all seemingly out of reach on her current graduate student budget. However, in the course of attending garage sales and visiting flea markets, she has acquired an assortment of aristocratic looking old chairs (second-hand reproductions) and an elegant but very worn dark wood daybed which she has elegantly draped with velvet remnants from discount fabric stores.

Then there is the dramatic silver candelabra she bought for almost nothing at an estate sale because it had numerous dents and scratches. Tanya spent a rainy afternoon cleaning and polishing it with old rags and a tooth brush while watching a favourite vintage film. It now shines brightly, the cracks, scratches and dents only adding to its patina. Several friends have asked her if it is a family heirloom!

While these objects are not precisely the things Tanya would choose for her dream house if money were no object, they are nonetheless beautiful and evoke a feeling of prosperity. Although she looks forward to refinishing and upholstering these objects or even replacing them in the future, she is enjoying her home furnishings now.

 Possibilities
Does your living space already reflect your preferences? What would be one simple and pleasing way to introduce or add some aspect of the things that bring joy into your home environment?

Fortunately, creativity and flexibility can help here. Creating a living space that reflects your preferences and therefore your Authentic Self can, but need not be, a financially costly project.

The Greek god of joy, Dionysus, was said to curse people with madness if they refused to honour him by participating in joyous rites. I have wondered at times if perhaps this metaphorical madness was intended not as a punishment, but as a means of release from rigid and preconceived patterns and ideas about life and lifestyle in order to reclaim the ability to be happy. Beware of all-or-nothing thinking when designing tranquility and beauty into your home; rigid thinking patterns can cheat you out of a daily pleasure that is rightfully yours.

This chapter has offered a variety of ideas for enhancing your enjoyment of everyday life at home. I encourage you to develop your own adaptations, one small step at a time. Taking positive action to enhance the quality of everyday life for yourself and those around you is an immediate aspect of the larger task we all share: creating a world where people feel cared for and in harmony with one another and the world around them. The next chapter focuses on the related task of creating a nurturing environment in your place of work.

Chapter Three
Enjoying Yourself
More at Work

How Sunday into Monday melts!

– Ogden Nash

As we reach the Millennium, people are spending more and more time at work. As a result there is increasing pressure to create work environments that enhance rather than detract from the quality of our life experiences. This chapter offers a variety of ways for you to make work a nurturing and life-enhancing experience.

Enlivening Your Work Space

Do you work at home, in an office, in a cubicle or somewhere else? Do you have physical space to call your own? If you have a specific area such as an office or a desk to call your own, how does this work space reflect your passions in life?

David was in charge of supervising my work many years ago at a small rural mental health clinic. I still remember the pleasure of walking into his small office on the Wednesday afternoons when I met with him.

Although situated in a dreary corner of a sterile hospital building surrounded by flat, treeless farmland, the interior of his office evoked his favourite area: the Pacific Northwest. The walls of his office were decorated with large colourful posters depicting the lush green fern forests and windswept beaches of the Oregon coastline.

At the far end of that same long, ugly institutional corridor where David worked, I shared a tiny windowless basement office with two women colleagues. One neurotic neatnik non-smoker (me) and two smokers with idiosyncratic filing systems occupying an inadequately sized space in a clinic with a history of political tension, we were prime candidates for conflict.

Nevertheless, we got along well. We managed to create a friendly environment within the impossibly small physical space we shared. We accomplished this partly through courtesy and partly by hanging brightly-coloured fabric prints on all the walls. But it was especially enhanced by a secret the three of us shared.

Behind our office door, and visible only to us, was a life-size poster of the gentleman of our dreams, Clark Gable, wearing an elegant tuxedo and beckoning us to the party of a lifetime. So vast was the contrast between the elegant world of Clark Gable and the one we inhabited in that nearly airless office, it was impossible to see that poster without laughing! Even years later as I write this, I find myself smiling. It reminds me of the value of bringing a sense of humour and playfulness to work.

 Possibilities

Does your work space reflect your personality and provide creative inspiration for you to do your best work?
What would be a small and easy thing you could incorporate into your work environment to enhance your physical or psychological comfort?

A Sense of Play at Work

Once a day and more often on difficult days, Alice opens her file drawer and gently strokes the fur of the teddy bear she bought several years ago for her nephew. It never made it out of her office. It's not that Alice doesn't like her nephew, she's bought him other teddy bears and many other toys as well. But Alice decided long ago that she would not part with this bear, the soft brown furry one she keeps discreetly in her file drawer. Why? Because something about that cuddly stuffed toy calms her nerves and soothes her when the demands of her job as a busy corporate executive approach an overwhelming level.

Lisa, a receptionist for a women's health care clinic, openly displays her collection of tiny stuffed animal toys on her desk. She has her employers' permission to do this, in fact they encourage it. The cuddly bodies and comical faces of the toys bring a smile to almost anyone entering the office.

Charlie keeps three small beanbag balls near his desk so that he can take a juggling break now and then. They are shaped like little televisions, and he says playing with them clears his mind and afterwards his concentration is better.

Brad, a talented advertising copy writer, makes good use of his shark hand puppet as a way to get past writing blocks. He says the puppet reminds him of some of his aggressive competitors in the business world.

Much to the amusement of his co-workers, when things get stressful in the office and he's having trouble writing, Brad "consults" with the shark, giving it a voice and a humorous perspective. Afterwards, he finds he can write again.

 Possibilities
Do you have any toys in your office?
If not, what might you enjoy?

Living Things Bring Life to Work

My dentist has a beautiful aquarium built into a wall in his reception area. Double-sided, it allows both staff and patients to enjoy the soothing colours and movement of the tropical fish as they glide through the sparkling water. I imagine it relaxes the people who work there as much as it does me.

As a psychotherapist, my office waiting area has been enhanced over the years by a series of well-behaved dogs and cats. My clients tell me they find the animals' presence comforting, and some people find it easier to talk while stroking a friendly furry body.

While some offices have rules against animals, their comforting presence can be felt with photos or paintings of animals.

If you have adequate light, a well-tended plant brings a bit of the outdoors inside. Personally I cannot resist the appeal of having at least one real flower on my desk during the summer, and a blooming plant during the cold months.

If your office doesn't have adequate natural light, a silk plant may provide the same feeling with minimal upkeep. Some people prefer the convenience and long-lasting quality of silk rather than real flowers as a way to have a beautiful bouquet every day.

 Possibilities
How can you best evoke the aspects of nature in your own work place?
What would be the easiest way to do this?

Your Loved Ones at Work

Lauren brings her two-year-old son to work. Well, not literally. She brings him to work through an ever-changing collection of photographs. Her desk also holds photos of her husband, parents, best friend and the teacher who always encouraged her. Just looking at the gallery of smiling faces helps her believe in herself. This is particularly valuable on days when the larger work environment is not as friendly and supportive as she would like.

Possibilities
Who would you like to be reminded of at work?

Their photographs will generate the same good feelings you experience in their presence. And if you wish to discourage unwanted romantic advances, a prominently placed photo of a spouse or fiancé is a discreet way to communicate that you are in a committed relationship.

Other Comforts

Do you use the telephone a lot at work? Richard found that spending hours on the phone was literally creating a pain in the neck until he purchased a headphone attachment. Available at telephone supply stores and office supply outlets, headphones also offer the advantage of leaving both hands free to facilitate note taking and other work during those times we all spend waiting on hold.

Maureen has a collection of beautiful silk pillows piled in the corner of her office. Reflecting her favourite colours, she also takes pleasure in their luxurious texture. The pillows lend a softening effect to the otherwise sterile office environment and provide helpful cushioning for her back muscles when she places one against the back of her chair.

An early riser, George gets to the office most mornings before it is officially open and the heat is turned on, and it is almost always freezing at that early hour. His daughter made him a knitted lap warmer which he uses until the place warms up.

 Possibilities
What special comforts could you add to your own office?

When Home Is also where You Work

Not everyone works in an office outside their home. Lisa, a computer specialist, does most of her work in a small home office. Since she has a space designated just for work, her ritual is simply leaving the room for the day and closing the door.

My office is at home, a cozy book-lined study overlooking a mountain meadow. The furniture is simple and spare and except for books and a small collection of framed photographs, the walls are bare. The real decoration is the tree-lined landscape outside. I know I have succeeded in decorating it in the right way for me because I enjoy working there.

But what if your workspace also serves another function within your home, such as a dining room or bedroom? How do you transform it to accommodate both functions without diminishing the effectiveness and aesthetic quality of the space? After all, you probably don't want to be thinking about work while you're eating dinner or trying to go to sleep.

Or maybe you do. Artists, writers and musicians sometimes get their best ideas and inspirations while going about the domestic activities of everyday life in the same place that they work. The challenge is to create a physical space that accommodates the necessity of moving from work to rest or play, and vice versa. If space is very limited, creating psychological rituals can mark your transition from work to play and relaxation.

Living and painting in the same studio apartment, Brad substituted rituals for walls to designate his transitions from work to play. Rising at dawn, he carries his breakfast out onto his tiny balcony to watch the sun come up as he sips his strong black coffee. This is his breakfast room because he keeps his painting supplies on the kitchen table. He marks the passage from work to relaxation by turning off the light over the kitchen table, lighting a candle and concentrating on his breathing for a few moments.

Ann, a musician who gives lessons from her living room, marks the end of work transition by taking a shower and putting on more casual clothes.

Tony, a physical therapist, sees patients in his home gym where he has a massage table. At the end of the day, he burns some sage incense so that the room will smell clean and fresh when he uses it to exercise the next morning.

 Possibilities

If you work at home, have you designated areas for business and recreation?

How do mark the transition from work to play?

The Travelling Workplace

Sometimes both our work environment and living environment are by necessity a hotel room. My lecture schedule causes me to spend several nights a month in hotel rooms far from home. Since I love to sew, I always bring a quilt to work on, a heating coil for making tea, teabags, a small candle and a bar of my favourite jojoba-scented soap. These things fit easily inside a small carry-on bag. The quilt helps transform an unfamiliar room into a place of warmth and comfort.

Whenever possible I purchase fresh local fruit for a quiet breakfast in my room. The details of familiar scents from home - soap and tea, the glow of a candle in the evening - help to transform a strange hotel room into place of warmth and comfort.

Consistency often helps, adding a note of relaxing familiarity to an otherwise strange environment. If you prefer a certain kind of pen or other writing implement, it is a good idea to use the same kind wherever you are. The same is true of paper and other office supplies.

You may have no specific office or studio or even hotel room in which you routinely work. Your work may entail constantly moving from one location to another. Fortunately, a work space of your own can be portable.

As a constantly travelling journalist, Ed has worked, eaten and slept in tents, trains, buses and boats, as well as in hotel rooms. More than anything else, Ed thinks of his Filofax as his workplace. Compact and portable, it is an external symbol of the very personal work environment that he carries with him everywhere.

Besides serving as his appointment book, the notebook contains maps, airline, train, and bus schedules, plastic pockets for credit cards and for pictures of family, friends and pets, phone numbers, vital work information and a supply of blank paper.

It also contains clippings of inspiring quotations from some of his favourite writers. Serving as a familiar touchstone, the act of opening his Filofax helps Ed focus his thoughts and make sense of the story developing around him amid the distractions of foreign or chaotic environments.

 Possibilities
What would be the smallest or least intrusive thing you could carry with your that would remind you of something that delights you and nurtures your spirit?

CHANGING THE EMOTIONAL ATMOSPHERE AT WORK

While it only takes one person to create conflict or tension in a work relationship, it usually takes two people to maintain it.

Patricia worked as a nurses' assistant in a large hospital. Her work required her to pick up several prescriptions each day from the hospital pharmacy. The hospital pharmacist was a rude older man who seemed to take an instant dislike to Patricia.

Even though the prescriptions were called into the pharmacy several hours before Patricia went to pick them up, the pharmacist never bothered to fill them until Patricia arrived. Even then he often kept her waiting while he filled the orders of other people who came in after her. He seemed to ignore her deliberately.

Since she had many other duties in addition to picking up the prescriptions, Patricia resented the time she wasted needlessly waiting in line at the pharmacy. When she tried to talk to the pharmacist about filling her prescriptions ahead of time, he always rebuffed her, telling her angrily that he was overworked and doing the best he could.

As the months went by, Patricia found herself staying later and later at work, trying to get everything done before she left for the day. She knew that one of the reasons she had to stay late was the time she wasted every day waiting at the pharmacy. Her resentment of the obnoxious pharmacist grew and grew. Thoughts of how much she disliked him began to intrude into her hours away from work. He was ruining the job she had worked so hard to obtain.

Patricia often talked to her mother on the phone, and told her about all the misery the horrible old pharmacist was causing her at work.

She also told her mother about the kindly old janitor who worked on the same floor as the pharmacy. The janitor always had a friendly word for everyone. Thankfully Patricia saw the janitor when she came out of the pharmacy each day. They liked to tell each other jokes, and he always cheered her up.

When her mother came for a visit that year, Patricia took the week off work. Towards the end of her stay, her mother ran out of a necessary prescription. Although she dreaded seeing the pharmacist on her vacation, Patricia offered to go to the hospital to have the prescription filled. Her mother declined. She wanted to go to the pharmacy herself and have a look at the pharmacist and the janitor her daughter had told her so much about.

The following day, after her mother left, Patricia went back to work. When she walked into the pharmacy, the old man greeted her courteously and told her that her prescriptions were ready. Patricia was so astonished that before she thought about what she was saying she had thanked him politely and wished him a nice day. The next day the prescriptions were ready and waiting for her, and this time the pharmacist wished *her* a nice day. Patricia was completely mystified by the dramatic change in his behaviour.

Patricia telephoned her mother and asked her what she had said to the pharmacist. Her mother had told the pharmacist what a wonderful job Patricia said he was doing and how seeing him always brightened her day. She added that after going to the pharmacist, she had passed that rude old janitor in the hall, and she knew just what her daughter meant, he really was an obnoxious man! She had not spoken to him, of course.

The courteous relationship continued between Patricia and the pharmacist until he retired five years later.

Replicating Patricia's mother's accidental intervention is unlikely, but perhaps there is something else you could do that would improve the psychological environment between yourself and your co-workers.

Peter works in a public agency fraught with political tension. His position as a liaison between various departments is funded by the federal government. His colleagues, however, must compete with each other for the ever-decreasing state and county fund for their programmes. This contributes to an emotional climate of distrust and hostility. As the one person whose job is not at risk because of statewide financial cutbacks, Peter should be a natural scapegoat for his colleagues. But he is not.

Several years ago, when he noticed tension building among his colleagues at work, Peter decided to do something to raise morale. He went home after work and spent half the night baking several dozen blueberry muffins. He brought them in the next morning and distributed them to every department without a word. Everyone wanted to know where the muffins had come from, but Peter refused to answer. He just smiled and said, "It's a mystery."

That afternoon several people who had not spoken to him for months greeted him in the hallway. Initially they talked about the mysterious muffins, but soon people from various departments began talking to each other.

Every few months Peter privately decrees it "mystery-muffin day", and brings muffins or other treats to work with no explanation. There has been much speculation about who made the muffins, and some people suspect Peter, but no one knows for sure. Meanwhile, morale among the agency staff members and relationships between the various departments has continued to improve.

Of course baking muffins can be laborious after a full day of work, and many people don't have the time. Ellen works in a large inner-city insurance office. The building is old and the fluorescent lights cast a sickly glow on the ugly brown carpet and worn leather furniture. In Spring and Summer she brings weekly bouquets from her garden.

Ellen gives one bouquet to the receptionist at the front desk that everyone passes when they enter or leave the building. She places the other bouquet on her own desk. Everyone comments on the beauty of the flowers. They stand out brightly because of their unlikely surroundings.

After Ellen started bringing the bouquets, a colleague started bringing in a surplus of tomatoes from his garden to share with co-workers.

Laughter has been proven to reduce the likelihood of contracting stress-related illnesses, and it can also contribute to reducing overall stress in a work environment. Ron regularly brings jokes and cartoons clipped from newspapers and magazines and posts them on the staff bulletin board at the engineering firm where he works.

One design firm contracts with a professional comedian, not to entertain the staff, but to lead them through gentle improvisational comedy exercises to reduce tension and thereby stimulate their mental flexibility and enhance their creativity.

Possibilities
Are you affected by tension or conflict in your workplace?
What is one small thing you might do to improve the emotional
climate where you work?

Changing Your Internal
Work Environment

Are you unhappy at work? If you have already done what you need to do
to make your physical environment and the shared emotional environment
at work comfortable, it may be time to work on your own internal
environment.

The Role of Self-Talk

Adam complained that he dreaded going to work. He had been feeling
this way ever since his company's expansion had necessitated a move to a
large modern building across town. Since the physical surroundings of his
office had changed, I assumed that there was something that he didn't like
about his new work space.

Maybe Adam could add something to his office or to his desk that
would elicit good feelings. When I suggested this, he told me, "The
environment where I work isn't the problem. It's the environment I have
going on inside me. I have to do something about my self-talk."

He explained that he began each day by telling himself, "I don't want to
be here." Throughout the day this phrase repeated itself in his mind, and
the more he thought about it, the more he resented being at work and the
less he accomplished.

Each day he was getting further behind. The days dragged on, each
feeling like a seemingly endless expanse of time. When he finally reached
the end of a work day, Adam left feeling guilty and tired. He was unable
to enjoy the hours of freedom he had because he knew he would have to
return the next morning.

The reason Adam didn't want to be at work was not that he hated his
job. It was, he said, "as good as any other job, and if I have to work, this is
the kind of work I want to do." The problem was that right now he didn't
feel like working, period.

It was Summer and he would rather be out on his boat, or spending
time hiking and going on picnics with his girlfriend, a school teacher who
had the Summer months free. Who could blame him? The trouble was, like
most of us, he needed to keep his job to support himself.

Adam was right about needing to change his internal environment, and
altering his self-talk was the first step. He decided to replace "I don't want

to be here" with "Well, you're here, idiot. Get to work." But this did not foster the internal environment that he was looking for: a positive state of mind.

When I asked Adam what he would say to a younger person with a similar problem, Adam said, "You'll feel better if you get to work." Asked to consider what difference repeating this self talk and behaving accordingly (returning his phone calls, completing his paperwork) would make for him, Adam answered, "I'd be able to leave at the end of the day not feeling guilty. I'd be able to enjoy my time off."

Adam wrote his new self-talk mantra "You'll feel better if you get to work" on a piece of paper which he taped to his desk where only he could see it. It took him about three weeks to eradicate the negative self-talk that had been polluting his internal environment, and afterwards he felt much better.

 Possibilities
What sort of self-talk do you experience?
Would it be helpful to change your self-talk? If so, what would be the best message to give yourself during the day?

Creating a Symbol to Centre Yourself

Elena's work as a professional mediator requires that she participate in tough negotiation sessions without betraying her emotions. Even when others lose their tempers, she always appears calm and cool at the bargaining table. Typically one of Elena's hands is at her side and the other is resting inside her jacket pocket.

What no one knows is that the hand inside her pocket is touching the seashell she always carries with her. Picked up on a beach many years ago, the seashell is ordinary-looking and conveniently small.

Touching it reminds Elena of the peace, immense power and vastness that she always experiences at the ocean. This affords her a calmness that helps her focus on the larger goals of her life and prevents her from, in her words, "sweating the small stuff".

 Possibilities
What object would remind you of peace and calm during the day?

If you have trouble thinking of an object that you could carry to symbolise this, ask yourself where and during what experiences in your life you have felt most centred and at ease. Then choose an object, photograph or quotation that reminds you of that experience and carry it with you into your work environment.

Relaxation, Yoga and Meditation

Erica enhances her internal environment by meditating. She posts a Do Not Disturb Sign on her office door once a day and meditates. When she closes the door, she also closes out all the tension of the day.

There are many ways to meditate. Erica prefers to repeat a single word, "calm" over and over until she feels her breathing become even and her neck and shoulders relax into what she calls her meditative response.

Carl finds that he accomplishes the same thing by taking time out to say a prayer. Jean mentally relaxes by imagining her thoughts projected on a blackboard. She envisions that with each breath she mentally erases the blackboard until she imagines it as a restful clear surface that leaves her with a calm, soothing feeling in her mind and body.

You may prefer to relax by focusing primarily on the sensations in your body. Liz finds that systematically tensing and then releasing the muscles of her body, beginning with her toes and progressing up to the top of her head, relaxes her best.

A long-time yoga practitioner, David takes a brief break during the day to go through his yoga stretching exercises.

 Possibilities

Do you have a favourite way to relax at work?

What would help you enhance your own internal atmosphere at work?

Finding Meaning at Work

There are at least three ways to make going to work a meaningful and rewarding experience. The first is the one that is usually talked about in self-help books: finding a way to get paid for doing what you love. Countless New Age gurus suggest that if people really do what they love, they will be good at it and the money will follow.

Unfortunately, given the current economy and the fact that some jobs are valued more highly than others, doing only work you love is not always a realistic goal. Doing the work you love may earn you money, but it may not be the amount you need to survive and live well. And even if your job already entails doing the work you love, chances are it includes some other duties as well. Within each person's chosen profession there are usually aspects of work that are less than enjoyable.

As a school counsellor Dee loves working with children and values having summers free to enjoy her own kids. She does not, however, enjoy the tedious record-keeping and test administering that her job entails. To cope, she focuses on the aspects of her work that she most enjoys.

The second way to find meaning and satisfaction in work is Big Picture thinking. Rather than concentrating only on the specifics of the job and constantly evaluating what you like and don't like about what you're required to do at work, Big Picture thinking invites you to examine the positive effects your work has on your own life and the lives of others.

For example, Suzanne's work at an airline ticket agency requires her to be at work before 5 o'clock most mornings. This causes her to miss out on many evening social events during the week. At the same time, her job has many perks. She gets to travel at a reduced rate, and part of the money she earns will help her to send her daughter to college.

On those icy mornings when going to work is a bleak prospect, she transforms the day into a meaningful experience by imagining her daughter graduating from college, and reminding herself of the trip she is planning for the Spring.

A Higher Goal

On another level, Suzanne finds meaning in her work by being competent and paying attention to detail, thus enhancing the quality of life for all the travellers with whom she interacts. This brings us to a third way to experience gratification in our work. The meaning of work and its potential rewards take on a very different quality if we look at work as a spiritual opportunity, as an effort dedicated to a larger and higher goal than our own personal well-being.

Many religions and cultures suggest that if you are faced with particularly difficult or distasteful work, it can be made meaningful and therefore more tolerable by offering your efforts up to God. This transcendent way of thinking does not have to be the sole territory of saints, mystics and spiritual leaders. Ordinary people may also be strengthened by focusing their daily efforts on a higher level.

Some people link the transcendent spiritual meaning of their work to a specific goal, such as making the world a better for future generations. As a result of his efforts as a civil rights activist, Nelson Mandela was incarcerated and forced into menial physical labour under inhumane conditions. Yet he found a sense of purpose by performing his daily labours in a dignified manner, believing that his actions added further credibility to the political stance he was imprisoned for espousing. He linked his work to a higher goal, that of winning freedom for people of colour in South Africa, now and for future generations.

Harold is a county employee whose job is collecting garbage in some of the rougher neighbourhoods of Chicago. Despite recent improvements in garbage collecting machinery, Harold's work is smelly, physically exhausting and often involves tolerating excessively cold as well as hot, humid weather.

Despite this, Harold often goes out of his way to pick up additional items people leave out for collection, doing more than his job description requires. He has been working in the same garbage collection job for twenty years, and has always enjoyed making the extra effort. He takes satisfaction in knowing his efforts make the city a better place for everyone.

 Possibilities
What helps you find meaning in the work you do?
Which of the three ways most support your work goals?
Notice what you are already doing that helps you accomplish this, and see if there is anything you could add or adjust.

This chapter has offered a variety of ways to enhance your quality of your life at work. The next chapter invites you to move beyond the realm of your work environment to explore your hopes and dreams.

PART TWO

·

CREATING A JOYOUS FUTURE

Chapter Four
Hopes and Dreams

Undoubtedly, we become what we envisage.

– Claude M. Bristol

This chapter will help you explore the cherished dreams, hopes and goals that you hold in the deepest recesses of your heart, creating the mind-set necessary to achieve your own unique version of them. At the highest level, this is not selfish nor in conflict with spiritual or religious teachings. In fact, loving oneself is a necessary condition for loving others and loving the world around you. As I write this, it seems that if ever there was a world in need of love, it is the one we are living in now.

The exercises in this chapter will help you reclaim the ability to identify deeply held hopes and dreams and to enhance or restore your ability to believe, in fact to expect, that good things can happen in your future.

If you have experienced numerous painful events, it may initially be difficult to imagine that a series of good things really could happen to you. Developing a belief that good things can happen to you and a mind-set based on the expectation that they will, is important because it allows the unconscious to create the psychological and behavioural conditions necessary to support and enhance the positive changes you desire.

Perhaps you're already well-acquainted with the hopes and dreams you cherish, or maybe at this point you are no longer sure what they are. Maybe some of your goals have changed. Or perhaps you've been so busy coping with your life up until now that you've lost track of or forgotten the hopes, goals and dreams that once shined so brightly for you. That was what had happened to Kate.

Moments after Kate walked through my office door I found myself feeling protective of her. A lovely young woman with gentle brown eyes and flowing dark hair, she focused her gaze primarily on the floor and spoke haltingly, as if she was used to being constantly interrupted.

Her slightly stooped posture, downcast eyes and nervous habit of twisting strands of her hair suggested that Kate had been through a lot in her thirty-odd years, and that she was feeling quite disheartened. This turned out to be true.

Sexually and physically abused as a child, rejected and blamed by the parents who should have protected her, Kate had endured a painful childhood. Then as a young adult she had suffered an excruciating divorce, cruelly betrayed by the man she had loved.

Now as a single mother, stuck in a job with an exploitative and obnoxious boss, she felt despairing of her life ever getting better. The only ray of sunshine in her world was her daughter Tamara. Thanks to Kate's mothering, Tamara was experiencing the once-in-a-lifetime kind of magic and wonder that comes with being five years old and in a loving home.

When I asked her how she would know that things were getting better in her life, she said: "I don't know. I feel completely overwhelmed. I don't even know what I want anymore. I can't even imagine it getting better. But it's got to. I can't go on like this."

Despite her joy in Tamara, other aspects of Kate's life were so miserable that she had contemplated suicide more than once. Fortunately her concerns about the hurtful effects this would have on five-year-old Tamara had prevented Kate from hurting herself.

I say, fortunately not only because her daughter needed her, but also because Kate's life would improve significantly, in fact far better than she could have imagined on the day we first met.

Besides, the world needs people like Kate. Kate is a kind and good person, a creative and sensitive soul who has a lot to give to other people and to herself. One of the saddest phenomena I have had to face as a psychotherapist is the frequency with which kind, smart, sensitive people like Kate are wounded by life's cruelties.

Despair sometimes prevents people like Kate from taking the actions needed to finally get the life they deserve, a life that will heal the pain they've been through and help them experience the joy of being alive.

If you've been through a series of painful life experiences, you sometimes feel hopeless and helpless. But don't be trapped into believing that you're going to feel that way for the rest of your life. Even when life seems overwhelming and impossible, it will not always feel that way. You can take steps, one at a time, to move your life in the direction you want.

A first step is to figure out what you want and to believe that it is attainable. The following Letter from the Future exercise will help you rediscover your own unique hopes and dreams, and reclaim a way of thinking that was stolen from many of us in childhood through trauma or abuse, or even through the educational process that often ridicules or punishes day dreaming. The following exercise, based on creative imagining, is among the most powerful in this book.

A Letter From The Future

This imaginative process is often consigned to the exclusive terrain of inventors, writers, artists, musicians and creative geniuses, but it is actually an inborn human ability that belongs to all of us. When we lose our ability to dream, we lose a lot of our potential for joy. Most of us could benefit from taking time to reclaim and strengthen this natural gift.

 One Small Step

Pick a time in the future (five, ten, fifteen, twenty years from now, or any length of time that is meaningful to you). Record the future date you have chosen at the head of your letter. Imagine that the intervening years have passed and you are writing to a friend. Choose someone with whom you would like to continue to be friends in the future.

When writing your letter, imagine that by the letter's date you are living a joyous, healthy, satisfying life. If there are problems with which you are now struggling, assume they have either been resolved or that you have found satisfying ways to cope with them.

Explain how you have resolved problems or difficulties that once plagued you. Describe how you did it, what you found to be most helpful from the vantage point of looking back on your life from the future. Be sure to include a description of how you spend a typical day in your future life.

Describe in detail how you spend your time in this imaginary future. Where are you living? Describe your relationships, beliefs, reflections on the past and speculations towards the more distant future.

This letter is not meant to be mailed. It is for you only. The purpose of dating the letter and writing it to a real person is to strengthen the psychological realism of the letter.

Here is a small part of the letter that Kate wrote:

27 January, 2010

Dear Sarah

Here is the letter I promised to write after Christmas.
This year has passed so quickly that I have not had time to

write very often. I hope this finds you well. I have been enjoying my work ever since I left my old job. I wake up each morning in a great mood. I have been able to maintain the weight I lost at Weight Watchers.

On a typical day, I get up early and in a good mood, do some exercise then wake up Tamara. I drop her off at school and I go to work. At night I either relax with Tamara, go out with a friend or do something creative. I am dating a very nice man. Tamara continues to be a great joy in my life. Life is good these days and I feeling lucky to be alive.

In writing your letter, don't worry about limiting yourself to things that seem realistic given your current life. This is not essential and may unnecessarily constrict you. Your Letter from the Future should be written with an open heart and an open mind so that you have room to surprise yourself.

John, for example, had lived all his life in a flat land-locked area of the Midwest. He was very surprised when he described himself in his Letter from the Future as living on the coast of Hawaii. Although this did not seem readily achievable when John was writing his Letter from the Future, he allowed himself to write about it anyway.

Writing his letter eventually led to some important discoveries about who he was, what he loved most and how to create more joy for himself. As a result, John had some remarkable adventures that he could not have anticipated before writing his letter. Years later, the experiences and discoveries that emerged as a result of his Letter from the Future continue to inspire him.

If for some reason you don't enjoy writing, you might dictate your Letter from the Future into a tape recorder. However, I have found over the years that this exercise tends to be most powerful when actually written. The psychological realism created by writing and dating an actual letter lend impact to the exercise. Take some time now before going further in this chapter to write your own Letter from the Future.

 Possibilities

Now that you have completed your letter, what did you learn?
What did you include in the letter that is not yet happening in your life?
What do you imagine would be the result of this happening?
What is the first step you might take towards your desired future?

Keep this letter in a safe and private place, where you can refer to it as needed.

After writing her letter, Kate told me, "It's only an imaginary letter, but I find myself feeling more hopeful. The letter seemed to give me the idea that things could get better. And after I wrote it, I realised that there were a couple things in it that I could do now, even before I get a new job." Kate's letter may appear to be more down-to-earth than John's, but the changes it eventually led to in her life were just as great.

As is usually the case, the immediate results of Kate's letter were small and gradual. Kate had a good week immediately after writing the Letter from the Future. Her face brightened as she explained to me that using her own letter for guidance, she had started her work day mornings more playfully with Tamara, much like she had envisioned in the letter, and she had hired a baby-sitter so that she could have dinner with a friend the following week.

But there was still a sadness in her eyes, and her shoulders seemed weighed down, as if she were still carrying the burden of some of the bad things that had happened in her past. But after a moment of quiet reflection, she blurted out, "I'm scared. Things feel a little bit better, but I'm afraid I'm going to lose sight of what I wrote about in the letter and it will all fall by the wayside, and I'll always be stuck in this job. I've tried to change before and it never seems to work. I don't carry through. I intend to, but I don't."

Kate had a good point. She had a right to be afraid. Change is hard, and it is all too easy to live a life based primarily on our fears rather than pursuing heartfelt hopes and dreams. What Kate needed now was a way to counterbalance the bad things that had happened in the past that were weighing her down. Otherwise she was in danger of losing sight of the different kind of future she was beginning to formulate in her mind.

Kate needed something that would make her new future even more vivid, so brilliant that it would be impossible to forget. She needed something tangible to hang onto to keep the dreams and goals that gave her hope and strength prominent in her thinking. Her next assignment, a Heart's Desire Collage, would serve this purpose.

THE HEART'S DESIRE COLLAGE

The Heart's Desire Collage will amplify the hopes and dreams you described in the Letter from the Future. Giving them a tangible representation will also strengthen their presence in your unconscious.

Collect symbolic items ahead of time by assembling photos, postcards, or your own drawings or images from magazines that remind you of your heart's desires. Pieces of paper, leather or fabric in your favourite colours are also useful because they will evoke the positive feelings you associate with various shades and textures. You may want to include objects from nature such as twigs, dried flowers or small shells.

You can also write words directly onto your collage. For example, when Kate made her Heart's Desire Collage, she added the words, "I deserve good things to happen. I deserve happiness."

One Small Step

Set aside at least an hour for this exercise. Where you spend this time is important. Make sure you have privacy or, if there are people around, that they are non-judgmental and supportive of what you are doing. You will need a piece of cardboard or heavy paper at least 8 by 10 inches, scissors, glue, writing or drawing tools and a collection of things that symbolise the hopes and dreams you began to explore when you wrote your Letter from the Future.

Now glue your collected objects onto the piece of cardboard. Arrange them in any pattern that pleases you. You can overlap or layer items, create a picture, or randomly paste things into a design that abstractly expresses your heart's desire for your future.

Take a moment to note what you have learned and how you feel.

Possibilities

What was it like to create a collage based on your own hopes and dreams?
What were you thinking about as you made your collage?
Stop and look at it. What does it tell you about who you are deep inside, beyond life's irritations, distractions and pain?

When making your own collage, remember that the goal is to rediscover the free and childlike imagination of your Authentic Self. That means that you are allowed to be playful and spontaneous, and it's fine to be messy. Don't be surprised if additional ideas occur to you while you're in the middle of making the collage. This is common.

Store your Heart's Desire Collage in a place where you will see it regularly, perhaps in a drawer where you keep everyday belongings.

If you are a typical Westerner, your Heart's Desire Collage probably included a number of possessions you would like to have in the future. Kate's did. Along with a picture of a woman sitting at a desk looking happy (to represent feeling good at work), snapshots of herself and her daughter and heart shapes to symbolise a future love, she also included a clipping of some wonderful white wicker furniture that she longed to have on her enclosed porch, and an image of a beautiful new car she had cut out from an advertising brochure.

There is nothing wrong with including material items in your Heart's Desire Collage. In fact doing so often indicates that you are making progress towards allowing yourself to feel deserving of the material things you want. It is a sign that you have moved beyond the negative mind-set that is typically created by experiencing painful life events. It is good to get what you want.

YOUR HAPPINESS

The next chapter is dedicated to helping you move towards your goals. Before we move beyond discovering what you want, to the specifics of how to make it happen, we need to talk about happiness.

We've all heard the phrase, "Money won't make you happy." While I've heard that said over and over again, I've heard the rejoinder just as often: "I'd like to be in the position to find out!" Most people associate possessing certain material belongings with happiness.

According to extensive research at the University of Chicago - excluding abject poverty in which people do not have adequate food, shelter and clothing to survive - there is no correlation between material wealth and happiness (Csikszentmihalyi, 1990).

The best and most succinct statement of the relationship between the heart's desires - material and otherwise - and happiness that I have found is something I once read on an antique sampler:

> *It's not how much we have, but how much we enjoy that brings happiness.*

Enjoyment is an ability that can be learned, and once learned, expanded upon. The final section of this chapter offers two exercises designed to enhance your capacity to enjoy the life that you are in the process of creating.

Cultivating the Gratitude Attitude
In her wonderful book, *Simple Abundance*, Sarah Ban Breathnach suggests that people keep a record of things for which they are grateful in a gratitude diary. This can be incorporated into your existing journal, or you could devote a special blank book to these entries.

Even if you don't go to the trouble of writing down what you are grateful for each day, asking yourself what you could be grateful for will have an encouraging effect because it shifts your way of thinking into a positive direction.

One Small Step
Cultivate your own Gratitude Attitude. Identify at least three
things for which you could be grateful. Think about three
beneficial things, and then notice what happens to your mood as
you do so. Repeat this exercise once a day for the next week, and
notice what happens after you identify the three, or more, things.
Notice how easy or difficult this is for you, and most important,
notice the effect this has over accumulated days.

Although it is not true for everyone, Kate found that listing the things
for which she was grateful fairly easy. The image of her beautiful little
daughter, her friends and the fact that she was healthy came to mind
immediately. Kate noticed that repeating her Gratitude Attitude list last
thing at night helped her relax and feel more peaceful as she drifted off to
sleep. When she did it first thing in the morning, she felt less intimidated
by the demands of the day.

Creating a New Influence in Your Life
Children learn by modeling. Later in life our ability to live a satisfying and
joyous life is still effected, for better or worse, by the people who have
influenced our thinking and way of living. Often the presence of these
people and their effects on our way of thinking and being happens
randomly or without our having much control.

This was certainly true for Kate, who observed after a week of making
her nightly gratitude list: "This is such a good thing to do. I told Tamara
about it and we have started doing it together as a little game before I put
her to bed at night. She loves it. I wish I'd had someone in my life to teach
me things like this. It may sound terrible but at times I wish I had different
parents because mine were not always a very positive influence on me.
They didn't put much value on enjoying their lives and their children, and
I'm afraid that has had a bad effect on me."

In the following exercise you will consciously choose a person who you
would like to have had as an influence on your life and to integrate some
of their wisdom into your consciousness. This exercise can counterbalance
other influences that were not always positive or helpful.

 One Small Step
Think of someone who embodies a way of living that you value, a
person you admire in some way. This person can be living or dead,
famous or unknown. He or she can be someone you know
personally or someone you are acquainted with only through
literature, movies or stories you have heard. If at all possible, find a
picture of this person (or draw one) to look at while doing this

exercise.

Write a detailed description of this person, emphasising the qualities that you most admire.

Think about why you have chosen him or her to be an influence in your life.

 Possibilities

What do you find most appealing about this person's approach to life ? How would this person respond to your current situation?

When choosing a person to be a new influence in her life, Kate thought of many people she had admired over the years, including her best friend's mother, Alma. But she realised that Alma would not be a *new* influence. Kate had already enjoyed a close relationship over many years with both Alma and her daughter, which had helped Kate create a loving relationship with her own daughter.

Kate surprised herself by picking Mr Stanley, her 7th grade science teacher as her new influence. She hadn't known him well, but had felt supported and encouraged by him in class. He was one of the few teachers she had in grade school or high school who encouraged girls to consider science as a profession. Kate sensed he had liked and respected her. He had believed in her abilities enough to encourage her to enter a scholarly science competition which she had won.

Sadly, Mr Stanley was now long dead. However, with this exercise the qualities she associated with him could become a more prominent influence on her current life. Although she chose him spontaneously and intuitively, Mr Stanley was a good choice for Kate. He embodied many of the values she needed to embrace before creating the life she needed and wanted. As a result, Kate would subsequently place more trust in her own intuition.

Here is a portion of Kate's response to the Creating a New Influence exercise:

> Mr Stanley was a kind person. You could just tell by the way he looked at you from behind those heavy old-fashioned plastic glasses. He was also very smart. I never saw him stumped by a question in class, and yet he was not at all conceited.
>
> If I imagine what Mr Stanley would say or do in my current situation, I imagine him quietly going about his business, but at the same time being very strong. He wouldn't put up with any nonsense from his students or anyone else, and I'm sure he wouldn't put up with any ridiculous demands from my boss.
>
> He had a way of talking that when he said something you

knew he meant it. Mr Stanley was also someone who never stopped learning new things. If he were in my situation he would be using it as an opportunity to learn. He'd be taking all kinds of new training whenever it was available, and eventually that would help him get a better job.

One Small Step
Think back to the person you chose as a new influence in your life.

Possibilities
How are you similar to the person you described in the Creating a New Influence exercise?
How are you different?
What is it about this person's approach to life that appeals to you?
What aspects of this person's lifestyle do you wish to incorporate into your own life? Are there any things that you are already doing that are examples of this? If so, what would be the effect of doing a little more of this in order to integrate this quality further into your personality?

If you feel you don't possess any of your chosen person's admirable qualities, what would be a small sign that you are beginning to incorporate such qualities? Consider a scale of 1 to 10, in which 10 meant you had succeeded in incorporating a new quality into your behaviour to the fullest degree possible, and 0 meant not at all.

What could you do that would raise it a half point or more? Experiment with enacting the behaviour you identified, noticing the difference this makes for you. Then identify the next small step and try that, and so on.

The first step Kate identified was to make a conscious effort to behave in a calm, unruffled way at work, as she imagined Mr Stanley would have done. She found herself behaving with a calm strength and self-assurance towards her boss. When she found herself being unfairly pressured by her boss or co-workers, she imagined Mr Stanley's face. She told me, "It's strange but I feel much more respected at work since I created the influence of Mr Stanley in my life. My boss seems to sense that I am stronger. He hasn't been trying to get me to work after hours anymore. It's almost like I've taken on some 'male energy' that helps me stand up for myself at work."

In the days and weeks to come, notice how the influence you created shows up in your own life. At difficult and challenging moments it may be helpful to imagine the face of your chosen person.

After beginning the daily Gratitude Attitude ritual, and completing the Creating a New Influence exercise, you should feel much stronger and more confident. You may be ready to tackle some of the additional changes from your Letter from the Future and your Heart's Desire Collage.

You have been building up your inner strength and self-knowledge as you have progressed through the exercises in this chapter. Before moving on, take a moment to appreciate what you have learned about who you are and what brings you joy.

CHAPTER FIVE
YES, YOU CAN!
TRANSFORMING HOPES AND DREAMS INTO AUTHENTIC REALITIES

Whatever you can do or dream you can, begin it.
Boldness has genius, power and magic in it.

– Goethe

This chapter will help you progress towards living the life you want in the future, teaching you steps that will eventually lead to a "miracle" in your life. One definition of a miracle is "a course correction" (Wapnick, 1989). In defining a personal miracle as a "course correction", I do not mean to exclude the spiritual aspect of a miracle, but rather to emphasise personal action as opposed to passive thinking or waiting. As Benjamin Franklin once observed, "God helps those who help themselves."

A MIRACLE BRIDGE

My early childhood was spent on an isolated rural peninsula of land separated from the mainland, reachable only by a 30-minute ferry ride across the water. On the mainland people could visit well-stocked grocery stores, acquire needed hardware, buy toys for their children, wool to knit sweaters and fabric to sew warm clothing needed for our rugged winters.

Regular boat trips were necessary because these essentials were not readily available on our little peninsula. As a child it seemed that everything we needed to make our life exciting and happy was available on the mainland.

Far too often the distance between the two peninsulas was insurmountable. Storms and high winds made the crossing so treacherous that the ferries were often cancelled.

I remember standing in our kitchen and looking out the window at the dark blue-grey water. As I saw the white-capped waves growing larger and larger, I knew I wasn't going on my long awaited visit to the five and dime store on the lower peninsula.

Fortunately, the problem of crossing the water was eventually solved with a bridge spanning the five-mile distance between the two peninsulas. Many people in our small town had scoffed at the idea that it was possible to build a bridge across two points so far apart. Consequently, after it was built, many people called it the "miracle bridge". The bridge changed life in our town, allowing people to live with greater ease and pleasure than before.

At some junctures, the things we want from life may seem just as unreachable as the mainland did from our small isolated town on stormy days. The exercises in this chapter will gradually empower you to create your own psychological Miracle Bridge to the life you've been wanting, incorporating your hopes, dreams and goals.

THE MIRACLE QUESTION

Kate was feeling better, but she needed more, she needed a bridge that would span the gap between the reality of the life she wanted and the constrictions of the life she had.

"I really like what I described in the Letter from the Future, and what I put into the Heart's Desire Collage, but it's hard for me to imagine exactly how I could make any of the bigger things happen, like getting a new job. Sometimes I feel like it would take a miracle to change the life I'm actually living into the life I really want."

The Miracle Question (invented by Steve de Shazer and Insoo Kim Berg at the Milwaukee Brief Therapy Center) is the first step to building a bridge to your desired future. It asks you to imagine and describe how a miracle in your life would look.

 One Small Step

Imagine that in the middle of the night, while you were asleep, a miracle happened and the problem or problems currently troubling you have either been resolved or you have found a satisfactory way to cope with them. Allow yourself to suspend any doubts, cynicism or scepticism, and simply notice what comes to your mind as you explore the fantasy of this miracle occurring. What would be different?

Since you were asleep when the miracle happened, when you woke up the next morning you didn't know it had happened. As you went through your day, you gradually began to notice signs that things were different, that the problems you had been struggling with the previous day were now resolved.

When Kate was asked the Miracle Question she didn't respond immediately. Then she began with the phrase she had used a lot in previous conversations, "I don't know ..."

To some people the words "I don't know" sound merely tentative, a disclaimer about what will follow. People often get into the habit of saying "I don't know" when their thoughts and feelings have been repeatedly discounted by others. This is particularly true when you have experienced a lot of invalidating responses from your parents.

As a psychotherapist I hear something else in those words. "I don't know" can be the magic phrase that allows you safely to dare to imagine things you would not otherwise consider.

Kate finally answered:" I wouldn't be working there anymore, and I wouldn't be getting up in the middle of the night worrying about the future."

Like most people, Kate's initial response to the Miracle Question was to identify what she *wouldn't* be doing after the miracle. As she struggled further to develop her imaginary miracle, I invited her to envision what new things she *would* be doing. After puzzling over this for a few moments, she thought of several ideas: "I would look forward to going to work. I would always be back home at 5.30 in the afternoon. I would play with Tamara when I got home because I wouldn't be so tired. Or if she was colouring I might clean up our house so it wasn't so depressing to look at. Actually, if a miracle happened, my house would already be clean and I would love the way it looked inside. I would have time to do creative things like painting watercolours or picking up my pen and playing with some lettering, like I used to do. And I would have lost weight. I would be slim and fit."

If you have not already done so, take some time now to answer your own Miracle Question. If you find it freeing to start with a disclaimer, you can began with "I don't know" and then continue your description. Remember to focus on the specifics of what *would* be happening rather than what wouldn't be happening after your Miracle.

The Small Signs of a Miracle
The next step is to figure out the first details that would indicate that your miracle had happened.

Possibilities
What would be the first small sign that your miracle
had happened?
What would other people notice in your behaviour that
would indicate that a miracle had happened in your life?

Beginning with her trademark, "I don't know..." Kate she was soon off
and running as she began to describe specific signs that the miracle had
happened: "I would wake up in the morning and I would be in a good
mood because I'd have a new job that I like. Since I would be in a good
mood, I would probably go into my daughter's room and wake her up in
an upbeat way. Maybe I would tickle her or make a joke or something. I'd
reach down and give her a little kiss on her forehead. I'm already doing
that a little bit more these days.

And since I was in a good mood, I would have got up early, so I would
have time to exercise on my stationary bike. I would ride my bike in front
of the TV while Tamara ate her cereal and watched *Sesame Street*. Tamara
would be surprised that I was exercising."

Making It Real
To make your Miracle a reality it is important to incorporate into your
everyday life one of the small signs you identified. Gradually, you can
then incorporate the additional changes one by one until you have built a
bridge to the Miracle you envisioned.

One Small Step
Start small, with one step, working one day at a time. Don't
overwhelm yourself as this could jeopardise or sabotage your
experience.
If such an action leads in the direction of your miracle then
continuing or increasing it will be the first step towards building
your Miracle Bridge.

People who repeatedly complain about a problem but do nothing about
it are often viewed as lazy. But what looks like laziness in unhappy people
is usually a fear of failure. Lacking confidence in their own abilities, they
are overwhelmed with the distance between the life they have now and
the life they want. The goal is to help you bridge this distance by reducing
it to a series of steps so small and gradual that you are *underwhelmed*.

I asked Kate if she could get up in the morning and kiss her daughter's
forehead and be playful with her, and then ride her stationary bike for a
while before leaving the house. She was clearly heartened and said, "Of
course I can do that. It doesn't seem like much. I'm already doing part of

that now with Tamara. Shouldn't I be doing more?" I explained the value of starting small.

By imagining small, active, observable signs of our personal miracle we identify achievable and non-intimidating behaviors that we can develop. Because these changes in behavior are modest and specific, you will be able to honour your commitment to doing them. And as sure as the sun comes up in the morning, these gradual behavioural changes will eventually lead to the bigger changes that complete your unique personalised version of the Miracle.

The Next Small Steps
When she returned the next week after setting the goal of incorporating two small signs of the miracle, Kate told me, "I feel better. Not fabulous, but definitely better. I can't say I love my life, but I dislike it less. Now what?"

 Possibilities
What would be the next small sign that would characterise your Miracle?

In Kate's case, she answered without hesitation, "I'd go on a diet."

I worried that going on a diet too quickly might be overwhelming in the face of the other life changes she was undertaking. Kate assured me it was not. She understood the gradual need to build a bridge of small signs to her real-life miracle. She planned to break the process of losing weight into a series of small steps. Since she had experienced good results with Weight Watchers several years ago, Kate decided that the first step would be to find out where meetings were held in her area. The next would be to attend one.

The following week Kate went to her first meeting and started the Weight Watcher's programme. She continued to ride her stationary bike. She also continued to wake up her daughter playfully each morning. "It sets the tone between us in a positive way for the rest of the day. We have both been joking more, and having a happier time together later in the day when I pick her up from school."

Two weeks later Kate reported that she had lost seven pounds and was feeling a lot less depressed about her job, even though she still hated going there. She also said she had more energy.

In subsequent weeks, Kate began practicing her calligraphy, started going out with a friend once a week and cleaned and re-organised her house. None of these actions directly related to the problem of her job, but they were things over which she had more immediate control.

After three months, Kate said to me, "I've got to start sending out CVs so I can get out of this job. It's such an obvious thing to do, I don't know why I didn't feel able to do it before, especially since it's the main thing I dislike about my life." She sat straight in her chair and her shoulders no longer stooped.

Mornings on the bike and weekly visits to Weight Watchers had paid off. She had achieved her goal of losing weight. Getting out of the house with a friend for an occasional night out had reduced some of the loneliness and boredom that had contributed to her depression. Kate was feeling better.

The idea of sending out her CV no longer felt overwhelming. She had the energy to do it now, and she also had the confidence to handle any rejections she might encounter during her job search. Her Miracle Bridge was now big enough and strong enough to support her safely over the rough waters that are part of job interviews.

When Kate's job search took longer than she had expected, she was able to persevere and eventually find a new job where she is treated with respect and fairness. And although finding a companion was not part of her original miracle, she has recently begun to date a kind, sensitive man.

Charting Your Progress
One of the advantages that Kate had in creating her miracle was that in working with me she had a witness for her progress, someone who could gauge how she was doing. Although it is possible to create your miracle without this, having someone to recognise your progress will help you stay on track.

If there is a supportive and non-judgmental person already in your life who would be willing to acknowledge and validate your progress, you could tell them some of the details of your miracle and invite them to be a witness to your small steps towards your miracle.

Unfortunately, supportive and non-judgmental people are not always readily available when we need them. And even good friends or family members who are otherwise accepting and kindly towards you may inadvertently become threatened by the idea that you are in the process of changing. They may directly or indirectly express well-intentioned scepticism or offer advice that could interfere with the momentum you are building in creating your Miracle Bridge.

If you do not have someone to reflect your progress, you can use the following device instead.

 One Small Step
Start by drawing a line with a mark or symbol at each end. Imagine that the mark on the left side indicates where you were on your Miracle Bridge before you answered the Miracle Question.

The mark on the right side indicates the point in your future when you are living the life you imagined in your Letter from the Future, your Heart's Desire Collage and your Miracle Question.

Now draw a vertical line on your Miracle Bridge to represent where you are now.

 Possibilities

What can you do to move yourself one step further along your Miracle Bridge?

What small step could you take, or continue, that would acknowledge your progress? Consider actions that could be completed in the next few days.

For example, at this point in her life, Kate has already accomplished many things that are part of the life she desires, but there are still other changes that would bring additional meaning and joy to her life. She would position herself on her Miracle Bridge here:

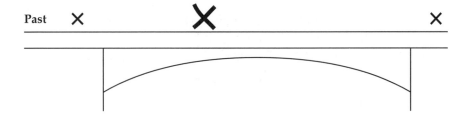

Refer back to your Miracle Bridge as often as needed in the coming days, weeks and months as you move through the additional exercises in this book to create the life you desire.

Creating a joyful life is a lifelong journey, and you can use the same Miracle Bridge for several years. Or you may prefer to apply the Miracle Bridge to shorter-term goals, and draw a new line for each new goal.

The Miracle Question can be used whenever you are feeling stuck or unable to imagine the solution to a problem. The Miracle Bridge is a tool to bypass the mental roadblocks that prevent you from moving beyond your problems and on to solutions.

The next chapter will focus on how you can use your relationship with time to further enhance your progress in creating the life you want.

CHAPTER SIX
TIME ON YOUR HANDS

Unlike other resources, time cannot be bought or sold,
borrowed or stolen, stocked up or saved,
manufactured, reproduced, or modified. All we can do
is make use of it.

– Stephen Rechtschaffen

Most of us spend half of our time wishing for things
we could have if we didn't spend half our time
wishing.

– Alexander Woolcott

How have you filled the space between now and when you first opened
this book? What has changed in your life? What has remained the same?
What is your relationship with time like? If your answer to the last
question was "I never have enough time," or "I have too much time on my
hands," you are not alone. Most of us seem to have a rather adversarial
relationship with time. There's never enough of it; it sometimes passes
without us realising it; and then some days, when we are waiting for it to
pass, it feels like there's far too much of it. How can we make time work
for us instead of *against* us? This chapter will tell you how.

The first section in this chapter will help you ascertain your own
perspective about time and identify the priorities in your life. The next
section offers strategies for gaining control of your time, enabling you to
spend it in ways you value. The final section invites you to explore the
rhythms of your body's natural clock and to experience the benefits of
"timelessness".

CHANGING PERSPECTIVES
ABOUT TIME AND YOUR LIFE

Recently, on a long trans-Atlantic flight, I was seated next to an attractive woman in her late sixties. As we chatted I was struck by the serene expression on her face, and her soft voice with its gentle Spanish accent.

There is something about being awake in the middle of the night while flying above a darkened ocean that easily invites conversation between two strangers. A few hours into the flight, as Lilliana and I gazed out of the window of the darkened cabin, we both commented with awe at the immensity of space above and below us.

Just as the moon rose from behind the clouds, Lilliana told me that she had been recently diagnosed with cancer. This was the second time in her life that she had been diagnosed with this disease. Before I could say anything, she stopped me. "Don't feel sorry for me. The cancer has taught me to make every moment of my life count. Life is a precious gift."

I asked how she was spending her time that made it count for her. Lilliana paused for a moment before answering, "It's not so much what I do, it's the *attitude* I do it with. I have these two sweet little dogs. Just enjoying sitting on the patio petting them is one way I make my time count. It's just a little thing, an everyday activity, but you see, I *appreciate* it. Time with my husband ... just being with him, doing ordinary things like eating a meal together, holding hands, reading in bed together, listening to the radio. These things make my life good.

"I know these things seem very ordinary, and they are. I used to do these same things when I was younger, before I had cancer for the first time, but it's like I wasn't really having the experience of them. My mind was always a little bit off somewhere else, always preoccupied, thinking of some project or chore or worry. Not now."

Lilliana noticed the tears in my eyes before I could blink them away, and continued, "I know it's sad to think about dying. It makes me sad to think that someday I'm not going to be around to pick up my baby grandson and cuddle him on my lap, and smell the spring flowers and talk to my husband, and my daughter and son. But we all die and that's not what's important to me right now. Enjoying being alive is what matters, and that's what I'm doing. Do you understand?"

Looking out at the night sky, we talked some more, and after our conversation had drifted to husbands, children and gardening, Lilliana and I both fell asleep. When I woke a few minutes before the plane landed, I told Lilliana what a gift it had been to talk with her.

I hope Lilliana beats the cancer again. Regardless of whether she wins her battle against the cancer, she is already succeeding in appreciating and enjoying the experience of being alive, fully using the time she has.

After meeting her, I found myself wanting to live more like the way she described - more in the present and more appreciative of daily life experiences.

The idea of confronting one's mortality as a way to more fully embrace life is not new. Plato advised, "Practice dying." In *The Teachings of Don Juan*, Carlos Castaneda describes the shamanic view of death as an ever-present companion and potential helper. Being consciously aware of the eventuality of death can help you stay focused on your goals, and maintain a meaningful perspective towards everyday life.

Practicing Dying

The following exercise will help you shift into your own wise perspective about how to spend the time you still have available in your life. Write your response so that you can refer to it afterwards.

One Small Step
Imagine that you have been told that you have only six months to live. Assume for the purposes of this exercise that although you have an incurable illness, thanks to the miracles of modern medicine you will remain relatively symptom-free and able to move around comfortably until the final moments of your life.

Possibilities
How would you wish to spend the remaining months of your life?
Who are the people you would want to spend time with?
How would you want to spend the time with them?
Which places would you like to visit or revisit?
Are there any specific things you would need to do to enhance a feeling of completion and peacefulness before you die?

Take a few moments now to examine your responses to the above questions; they hold valuable clues to how you might best prioritise your time and more fully honour your most heartfelt longings and needs. What is the first small step you could take to incorporate these changes into your daily life?

When Nancy came to see me for psychotherapy she described herself as being in the middle of a mid-life crisis. She was experiencing a pervasive dissatisfaction with her current life and was unsure about what she wanted for the future. Asked how she would spend her time if she knew she had limited time to live, Nancy first emphasised what she wouldn't do, "I wouldn't spend so much time worrying."

Asked what she would do *instead* of worrying, the following ideas came to mind: "Okay, so if I knew I had a limited time to live, what would I do instead of worrying? I'd take more walks. I'd play with my dog. I'd look at more sunsets. If I wasn't worrying, I'd have more time, so I'd tie some fly fishing lures just because it's fun to do. I'd spend more time with my husband hiking and bicycling in the woods just because it makes us happy to spend time together that way. I'd paint watercolours. And I guess I would put my belongings and legal papers in order so that when I died my husband wouldn't have too much difficulty sorting things out. It would be a relief for me too to have these things in order."

Nancy continued to talk for a few more minutes about how she might live her life differently if she knew she had limited time left. Then she paused, and looking at me solemnly said, "Yvonne, we *all* have limited time to live. It's just that we usually don't know exactly how long. You knew I was going to realise that when you asked me this question, didn't you?"

A Symbol for the Time of Your Life
This exercise will help you discover your own unique symbol to remind you to live fully and give priority to the things that really matter to you. Read the instructions completely before doing this exercise.

 One Small Step
Find a comfortable place to sit where you will not be disturbed for the next fifteen minutes. Concentrate on your breathing until you achieve a comfortable rhythm and feel centred in your body. Now close your eyes and ask your unconscious to give you a symbol that will remind you to spend your time in satisfying and heartfelt ways.

Sit quietly and notice what comes to mind after you ask yourself for a symbol. It may be an image, words or a feeling. Once you know what it is, write or draw your symbol so that you will remember it in the future. Afterwards, place it somewhere you will see it often.

Having your symbol readily visible to you will help you regularly reconnect to the idea that your life is by necessity time limited and therefore precious and valuable.

As time goes by, notice the effect that seeing this symbol has on your daily decisions about how you spend your time.

At the end of her therapy session, Nancy told me that had learned something important about the nature of how she now wanted to live her life, but feared that she would eventually lose track of this awareness. She said, "It's strange, but if I can just remember that I am going to die someday, I know that I'll be able to worry less, enjoy myself more, feel the relief of having organised my stuff. All that would feel so good. But I don't know how to keep from forgetting that I'm going to die someday. How can I keep from forgetting this? I really need to remember it."

I asked her what she might use as a tangible symbol of the inevitability of death.

Nancy paused and took a deep breath before answering, "Well, one thing would be I could paint a little sign that said, 'You're going to die!' and hang it on my bathroom mirror, but that feels too weird, and it would probably scare other people. A little skeleton would work, or even a little plastic skull like I've seen at novelty stores. Actually, I like the skull idea. I'm going to get a little plastic skull and put it right next to my night table, because when I'm going to sleep at night is one of the times I do most of my worrying. And then when I wake up in the morning, the skull will be there to remind me to plan my day in a way that includes at least some of the things I would do if I remembered that I only have a limited time to live. I hope the skull won't freak my husband out!"

I suggested that Nancy explain to him what the skull symbolised for her.

A year later, I ran into Nancy in the local grocery store. She told me she is doing well. In fact she said, "I've been having the time of my life." The skull is still in place on her night table. When she travels away from home, Nancy takes the skull with her so that she can place it next to her bed. Over the past year she has painted some wonderful watercolours, had some great times with her husband, and she says that when the snow and cold sets in this winter she plans to get her papers and belongings organised.

MAKING TIME
WHEN YOU DON'T HAVE TIME

My women friends and I have a common phrase that always makes us laugh: "in my spare time." Like me, most of my friends juggle multiple roles and are rarely idle. And yet my busiest friends are a living testimony to the saying, "If you want something done, ask a busy person."

Several times a year I take a day off to attend a quilting seminar. These are strictly hands-on experiences. You bring your sewing machine, sit at large tables with other women and sew various shapes and patterns under the guidance of an instructor. The idea is for each student to begin making a new quilt in the class and to finish it in the subsequent weeks and months. For people who love to make quilts, beginning a new one is a joyous and replenishing experience.

Guilty feelings are common among the students attending these quilting classes. Typical examples are: "I really don't have time to be doing this because I should be at home cleaning my house," or "I should be at my office because I've got a mountain of paper work." Fortunately another person in the seminar, usually an older woman with a wealth of life experience, inevitably responds with compassion and wisdom to these expressions of guilt: "That's probably exactly *why* you need to be doing this. You need a break from all those things. Stop feeling guilty!"

Getting Control of Your Time

If you don't already own a daily calendar with lots of room to write, get yourself one! Allocating time for the things you love is necessary when creating a joyous life that outshines painful or traumatic past experiences. Scheduling the things that really matter to you may be the only way that you will do them.

Even with a daily calendar to help you organise your schedule, allocating time for people and activities that matter to you may be difficult. Sometimes the only way to make more time is to simplify things or alter the way we approach regular tasks.

When caring for her orchid plants became a time-consuming duty instead of a source of joy, Ellen gave them away. Her friends were delighted to receive the orchids as gifts, and Ellen is equally pleased to be free of the chore of caring for them.

Once a perfectionist housekeeper, Sarah elected to have a less-than-pristine house so she could spend more time enjoying her young children. Reflecting on this, she observed, "I can always clean my house. The dirt won't go away, but my children aren't always going to be young and at home with me. I want to enjoy this time together while we can."

Marlena's favourite way to create more time in her life is something she calls multi-tasking. In between loads of laundry, she returns phone calls, pays the bills, prepares dinner and crochets afghan blocks. While not everyone would find this approach appealing, Marlena swears it makes her mundane chores more interesting, and allows her to accomplish much more in less time. As a result, she has more time available to do the things she most enjoys: gardening, taking long walks and playing card games on her home computer.

 Possibilities

What are the things in your life you wish you had more time for?

Are there tasks you might consolidate or eliminate to free yourself for the other things that you value or especially enjoy?

Uncluttering Your Life

Giving away items you no longer use to friends and charities clears out the clutter that can slow down even the most basic and necessary daily routines. How much easier and faster would it be to get dressed in the morning if your closet no longer contained those items you rarely or never wear? What about those old shoes at the back of your closet? Either repair them or discard them.

Are your kitchen cupboards so crowded with duplicate versions of utensils, pots and pans that finding what you need to prepare a meal has become a frustrating and time-consuming process?

Sometimes recycling is as simple as packing up a cardboard box with the kitchen items you no longer need and giving it to the young person who just moved into their first flat. They will be grateful, and so will you every time you put things away in your newly spacious cupboards.

What about the decorative items in your house? Has your taste changed since you acquired certain objects? Perhaps the picture you once loved no longer brings you joy. Maybe you've been hanging on to an ugly candelabra all these years, even though hate it because someone told you it was valuable. Perhaps you know someone who would love these things. Why not give these objects away and enjoy the pleasure you see on the faces of the family or friends who receive them.

Or perhaps it's time for a garage sale. One person's trash is usually someone else's treasure. You will make some money while gaining space and added simplicity in your life as your unwanted belongings find new homes. Of course some of the things that clutter and complicate our daily lives are too valuable or meaningful to be disposed of to strangers attending a garage sale.

If you have designated various belongings to people in your will, you might give some of those items ahead of time. A gift that comes from you *now* will hold richer memories for the recipient.

Every time I prepare a holiday meal, I am warmed by the memories connected to an old silver serving spoon I was given by my grandmother. I was thrilled and so was she because, as she told me at the time, she was relieved to no longer have the responsibility of keeping it polished! Giving things to loved ones while you are still alive means that they will remember your life rather than simply mourn your death.

When making choices to simplify your life beware of discarding items that hold such sentimental value that they are irreplaceable. Examples might include your baby's first lock of hair, your grandfather's shaving mug, the special card your mother gave you when you graduated, the pearl pin from your best friend. With the exception of those things that truly touch your heart, a good rule is never hang on to a possession that is neither useful nor pleasing to your eye, hand or ear.

Following Your Internal Clock

In his ground-breaking book, *The 20-Minute Break*, Ernest Rossi describes Ultradian rhythms, the 90 to 120 minute cycles that most of our bodies follow. From our physical energy, appetite and sexual feelings, to our creativity, mental alertness and emotional states, we are moving constantly through a wave-like cycle of activities followed by short periods when our mind and bodies seek rest and renewal.

Signals that we have reached the time to take a break and allow our body and mind to recharge include difficulty concentrating, memory loss, hunger, sleepiness, errors and moodiness. If instead of taking a break at these moments, we ignore and push through the period when our mind and body are crying out for rest, the resulting stress can lead to a host of psychosomatic illnesses, as well as increased stress and fatigue.

Drinking endless cups of coffee, smoking cigarettes and eating sugar-laden foods are typical ways to override our natural need for a few minutes of rest and renewal. Next time you have a craving for one of these, try allowing yourself to take a short rest break instead. Afterwards, notice whether you still have the craving for caffeine, sugar or nicotine.

Your Natural Rhythms
The following exercise will help you to learn about your natural Ultradian cycles.

 One Small Step
Carry a small notebook around with you for three days. Once an hour, during your waking hours, record your level of alertness and energy on a scale of 1 to 10.

Imagine that 10 means you are at your most alert level for working. At 9 you are still alert, but not able to concentrate as effectively as at 10. The midpoint 5 indicates you are neither particularly alert nor especially sleepy, a sort of neutral level. The lowest level, 1, signifies you are feeling so sleepy that it is difficult to stay awake.

Compare your hourly scores for three days to get a good idea of your natural high and low energy rhythms. This will help you organise daily activities to best take advantage of the times when your concentration and energy is especially high and to rest and replenish yourself during your low energy periods.

While a twenty-minute break is ideal, shorter relaxation breaks are also beneficial. Your break at work can be as simple as sitting quietly at your desk with your eyes closed for a moment, taking a walk to the water cooler, eating a piece of fruit or closing your door for a ten-minute nap.

As you continue to pay attention to your natural Ultradian rhythms, you will eventually be able to accurately estimate the time of day by how you feel physically and mentally instead of looking at your watch. Your body has a wisdom of its own.

Learning to honour one's inner clock will not only lead to enhanced productivity, creativity and concentration, it will also help prevent illness and fatigue. I have found that if I honour my Ultradian rhythms, I accomplish more yet feel less fatigue at the end of the day.

Since our personal rhythms do not necessarily coincide with those of our children, partners or friends, certain compromises are required. I do my best mental work first thing in the morning. My husband is a night owl and works well late in the evening. We have learned to adjust to one another's rhythms. He refrains from discussing complicated ideas or problems late at night, and I wait until the afternoon to discuss important decisions with him.

Timelessness: Taking Time to Do 'Nothing'
A friend who meditates describes an experience of timelessness - a little glimpse of eternity, or what it might be like to have time stand still. An advanced practitioner of Buddhist meditation, unless he sets an alarm or looks at a clock afterwards, he has no idea whether he has been meditating for five minutes or sixty minutes. The nature of those ecstatic experiences are so compelling and rewarding that time becomes irrelevant.

Although I have regularly practiced various kinds of meditation and centring techniques for the past twenty years, I have rarely had the experience my friend describes. Usually I am all too aware of time passing as I try to clear my mind of distractions. But I know what he is talking about, because I have experienced that sense of timelessness or time distortion when I am doing something that I love. For me it is usually gardening.

My husband and I live in a rural area overlooking a valley in the foothills of the Colorado Rocky Mountains. For seven months out of the year, I cannot resist beginning every morning with a walk through the garden listening to bird songs, discovering which flowers have opened and finding out which new seeds have finally sprouted tiny green leaves.

Sometimes an hour, or even two, pass before I come back into the house, but it always feels afterwards as if I have only spent a few minutes outside. Over the years, this seemingly everyday activity of walking in the garden doing nothing has become an ecstatic experience for me, a little glimpse of the boundlessness of eternity.

We all need to listen to our internal clocks so that we know when to work and when to replenish ourselves by doing nothing.

One Small Step

Take a moment now to consider the next twenty-four hours. Schedule a half-hour break in the next day or evening in which you are not expected to do anything except relax and replenish yourself.

During this time off you are to do nothing except what pleases you, whether it's soaking in a bubble bath, reading a magazine or simply resting. Afterwards notice what difference taking this break made to the remainder of your day.

If you feel you are too busy to do this, schedule a fifteen-minute break. But frankly if you are too busy to give yourself a half-hour break, what you probably really need is a two-hour one!

Taking time off to do nothing for a little while every day is not a luxury, it is a necessity. Paul, a busy young attorney, unfortunately had to learn this truth the hard way. Working in a high pressure job in a large legal firm, Paul had been putting in sixty and seventy hour weeks for over a year. Other than eating and sleeping, all his time was spent at his office working, trying to satisfy several very demanding clients. Paul knew that if he kept up this pace for another year, he would be made a partner in the firm.

And then it happened. Paul found himself sitting at his desk feeling terribly ill, unable to string one coherent thought together, despite the pressure of yet another deadline. No matter how he tried, he could not concentrate on his work.

Terrified, Paul called his doctor. He was admitted to a mental hospital that same night. He just couldn't think, and this caused him to believe he was losing his mind.

Paul was not losing his mind, his mind was shutting down so that sanity and the normal functions of healthy living could re-emerge. Fortunately, Paul listened to the message inherent in this experience and immediately began to slow down so that he could make time for a life outside of work.

Eventually Paul did become a partner in the law firm, but by then his work was no longer the only important thing in his life. He learned to savour friendships, hobbies, travel and relaxation, and to listen to his body's natural rhythms and needs, which in the long run probably lengthened his life. Paul has learned to organise his life with more respect to his internal clock.

A Child's Perspective of Time

Because their awareness is focused on the present, young children and babies offer their own particular gift to those of us who sometimes lose the knack of staying aware of the current moment. Children are very good at noticing what is around them and are more than willing to touch, taste and smell whatever is within their reach with fearless abandon. Parents sometimes describe the experience of seeing ordinary objects as if for the first time as they vicariously enjoy their child's appreciation.

 One Small Step
Think of an occasion when your attention was pleasantly absorbed by a baby or young child, when time seemed to stand still or pass effortlessly.

 Possibilities
How was this experience different from your everyday life?
How might you benefit from incorporating some aspect of this different sense of time into your daily life?
How might you do this?

Spending Time with Pets
I cannot end this chapter without mentioning animals and the transformative quality they can bring to the way we experience time. Numerous studies have shown that people who spend time with pets have fewer heart attacks, lower blood pressure and a more positive psychological attitude.

Just observing a pet enjoying himself is relaxing for most people. Perhaps this is because, like babies and small children, animals live in the present. They are not prisoners of the clock or hostages to work deadlines, and their presence is a reminder that we do not need to be either.

You may own a pet, or maybe the wild birds or the playful squirrels outside your office window are the only animal life in your world. Regardless of where they are, the animals that are part of your daily life can serve as potent reminders of the importance of being aware of your own natural senses as you go through life, savouring the moments as they pass. Take a moment now to think about the animals that are currently part of your life. Note how their presence can help you experience the beauty and gifts of the present.

This chapter has offered many ideas for enhancing your relationship with the time that belongs to you. Time will inevitably pass, and it is your right and privilege to spend time and experience its passage in the ways that are most meaningful and rewarding for you. Particularly if you suffered painful or traumatic experiences in the past, it is important to remember that as long as you are alive there is still time available to nurture yourself and create rewarding new experiences that can make the present more compelling than the past.

The next chapter will provide a variety of ways for you to enhance the current relationships in your life.

PART THREE

·

RESPONDING TO
LIFE'S CHALLENGES

Chapter Seven

Partners, Parents, Kids and Extended Family

Oh, life is a glorious cycle of song,
A medley of extemporanea;
And love is a thing that can never go wrong;
And I am Marie of Roumania.

– Dorothy Parker

When your own life is in order, you feel better about
yourself which makes you more clearheaded about
your marriage.

– Michelle Weiner-Davis

Enjoying a good relationship is an important part of creating a satisfying life. And while anyone who has suffered a painful divorce can confirm that being in a relationship is not always wonderful, it often is. Happy times from past relationships nurture many of the hopes and dreams we bring to new relationships. This chapter will promote your ability to have a great relationship.

The first section explores ways to enhance and strengthen relationships with a partner. The next section focuses on parents, siblings and extended families, followed by a section on relationships with our children. The final section offers guidelines for protecting yourself from exploitative and abusive people.

THE COUPLE RELATIONSHIP

For many people, a long-term couple relationship offers the greatest potential for joy, pain and growth. If you suffered emotional pain or abuse in the past, and have not yet experienced the counterbalancing effects of a caring and loving relationship, you might feel tempted to avoid the hazards and emotional intimacy of a future relationship for fear of being hurt again. Don't. The rewards of loving are more than worth the risks.

Complementarity: The Attraction of Opposites
Assuming you are in a couple relationship as you read this, are you and your partner exactly alike? I doubt it. A primary relationship with no differences between the partners could quickly become dull and boring. The disparate personality traits that initially attracted you to your partner are part of what keeps a long-term relationship interesting.

There is an ecology underlying the choice of a partner or spouse. We tend to choose people whose traits and abilities fit with but also balance ours. Positive complementarity is a term family therapists use to describe relationships in which the personalities and abilities of each partner fit together in a way that benefits each person and enhances the relationship. Such complementarity is at the core of many great relationships.

Judy and Michael have been married for thirty years, and they still delight in each other's company. Raised on a farm in the rural south, Judy grew up in a family where simple country pleasures were valued. Michael grew up amid the hustle and bustle of New York City in a cultured, intellectual family who "talked about wonderful ideas ad infinitum but usually never got around to doing much". Judy's earthiness, practicality, humour and country common sense were refreshing for Michael. At the same time, Judy was attracted to Michael's sophistication, love of the arts, and romantic "city gentleman" manners. Michael is a gourmet cook. Judy doesn't cook at all, but she grows gorgeous tomatoes, lettuces and other vegetables that Michael enjoys using in his cooking, and she loves what he cooks. Michael doesn't garden, but he really likes it that Judy does.

Evidence of complementarity is not always as blatantly obvious as it is with Judy and Michael. The best evidence of positive complementarity in a couple relationship are experiences in which the partners take mutual pleasure in each other's company. The more often a couple shares common pastimes, the more likely they will feel they have a good relationship.

Every relationship experiences positive complementarity at times, and the degree of complementarity in your relationship can be augmented. The following exercise will show you how to identify and increase the frequency of positive complementarity in your relationship.

One Small Step
Think of a time when things were going well between you and
your partner; you were both happy in each other's company, fitting
well together as a couple. This was an instance when you were
experiencing complementarity in your relationship.

 Possibilities
What contributed to this time of complementarity?
Where were the two of you?
What were you both doing?
When did it occur?

Now consider replicating some or all of those conditions. What would
be the first small step? Take that step. Remember, it is not necessary to
repeat exactly what you did on your special occasion. Your goal is to
capture the essence of the experience.

Marilyn and Ted recounted an idyllic vacation they spent together in
Mexico a few years ago, a time when they delighted in each other's
company. They walked along the beach, visited interesting restaurants,
gave each other back rubs, had great sex, listened to the sound of the
ocean in bed at night and read books that they loved. Right now, they have
neither the money nor the time to visit Mexico. But they could replicate
one or more of the aspects of the experience, thereby rekindling the
experience of complementarity they enjoyed there.
    They could walk outdoors together. Although the beaches of Mexico are
far from their Cincinnati home, they can still go for a walk near a lake or
river or some other beautiful outdoor setting. They might play a tape of
ocean sounds in their bedroom and listen again to the soothing sounds
they heard in their hotel room. Or they could go to a new restaurant in
their home town without their children. This would recapture some of the
novelty of visiting new restaurants in a distant country.
    Other possibilities include visiting a bookstore or library together to
rekindle their shared love of reading, going to bed early so they aren't too
tired to give each other a back rub or enjoy lovemaking.
    The next section will help you cope more easily with the difficult times
that occur even in the best relationships.

The Relationship Resource Inventory, or Remembering the Good Times, Especially when You're Having a Bad Time

Recently, my husband and I were sitting in our back garden watching the
sunset after enjoying a good meal. I was feeling especially appreciative of
something he had done earlier that day, and my feelings of love and

gratitude for him and our relationship were overflowing. I told him so. He really liked hearing this. Then he smiled meaningfully and said, "I hope you will remember this the next time you're mad at me." I knew what he was talking about. It's the unfortunate truth that the times we most need to remember the strengths and values of a relationship are when it's hardest to do so.

People tend to edit their storehouse of memories to support a current mood (Synder and White, 1982). When things are going well in a relationship, you are more likely to remember other happy and rewarding times with your partner. But when you're in a bad mood and irritated with your partner, you are more likely to recall troubled memories of difficult times between you, ignoring the good experiences you've shared. This can lead to further frustrations and outright conflict, and is typically how arguments between partners escalate.

The next exercise, The Relationship Resource Inventory, will promote good feelings about your relationship. Afterwards it can be used as a psychological "safety net" to prevent you forgetting the good things.

You can reread the Relationship Resource Inventory whenever you are feeling discouraged or frustrated with your partner, and want to approach a problem with a positive attitude. Therefore, you should respond to the questions in terms of what your partner does, as opposed to what he or she does not do.

 One Small Step
List the behaviours or personality qualities about your partner that you most appreciate. Now record shared activities that you enjoy. Provide as much detail as possible.

While you may not feel like rereading your Relationship Resource Inventory list when you and your partner are having trouble, it's worth making yourself do it anyway. As Michele Weiner-Davis points out in *Divorce Busting*, when making an effort to improve your relationship, "You don't have to like it, you just have to do it."

Remembering the strengths of your relationship when you are confronting a problem helps keep it in perspective, so that its significance doesn't get blown out of proportion. It's easier to solve a small problem than a large one.

Now that you've completed your Relationship Resource Inventory, how do you imagine your partner would react if you showed it to him? What do you think your partner would write if he were to create a similar list? Whether you decide to share your Inventory with your partner or not, the emphasis you placed on acknowledging admirable aspects of your relationship will positively colour your attitude and optimally influence any future disagreements.

A Sense of Self, Separate from Relationships
Initially it may seem paradoxical to include a discussion about the need to develop a sense of yourself, separate from relationships, in a section about couple relationships. However, lack of a "sense of self" independent from the relationship can wreak major havoc. People with no sense of self separate from the relationship are in the terrible position of expecting their partner to meet all their emotional needs. This places an unrealistic burden on the relationship and can lead to endless frustration and mutual resentment.

As David Schnarch points out in his excellent book, *Passionate Marriage*, a sense of self and the ability to soothe and comfort yourself independent of your significant other is crucial in order to create a fulfilling long-term relationship. This differentiated sense of self allows partners to build a relationship based on love and strength, rather than on feelings of inadequacy and dependency.

In my early thirties I went through a lot of pain at the breakup of a marriage. I feared that I would never love or be loved by anyone again. Worse yet, when my husband left I felt a terrifying emptiness that seemed to eclipse all sense of myself. The pain and terror of those first few days was a revelation. I remember thinking, "I never knew it was possible to feel this much pain."

What I experienced back then is an example of what can happen to a primarily undifferentiated person when their partner leaves. With the awareness that the marriage was over, I felt as if the person I was while I was married had now ceased to exist, and so had much of the familiar sense of how I defined who I was. It was ghastly.

The first few weeks after my marriage ended seemed like an endless "dark night of the soul". While everyday activities - such as work, self-care and conversations with other people - offered a measure of relief, being alone plunged me back into an agony of grief and self-doubt.

I was puzzled and somewhat crushed by the fact that my soon-to-be-ex-husband did not seem to be experiencing anything near the soul-shaking level of pain and anxiety that I was. He was already in a new relationship and seemed to be comfortably re-organising his life while functioning as usual at work and in his everyday life. Though I did not think of it at the time, already being in a new relationship may well have been responsible for some of his apparent resilience. Or perhaps he was simply far more differentiated than I was.

There are many different ways that undifferentiated people resolve their agony when a significant loved one leaves or dies. Some people rebound quickly into a new relationship. They may immediately feel better, confirming the suitability of their choice.

Other people immediately jump from one relationship to the next, denying themselves the opportunity to develop a sense of profound and permanent relief and stability. They remain undifferentiated and unaware of the peace and comfort they carry within themselves.

Others simply shut down emotionally and do not allow new relationships to become deep enough to risk the kind of loss they felt before. These people tend to keep others at arm's length.

But some people endure the anxiety of confronting their lack of differentiation long enough to develop a more stable and comforting sense of self that will stand them in good stead in future relationships.

After several long months the turning point in my own struggle with differentiation came quite unexpectedly, during a visit from a good friend. After listening quietly to my tale of woe, he offered the following advice: "Figure out who you are apart from all relationships and you'll feel better." While I had no idea how to do this, the notion stayed with me.

After my friend left I began asking myself at odd moments who I was apart from all relationships. Once I got over the initial anxiety of not immediately knowing the answer, the practice of asking the question began to evoke a sort of meditative state characterised by a growing sense of internal peace and comfort.

I began to realise that just asking myself this question meant I had some sense of self separate from all relationships; yet paradoxically it also meant that there was something bigger than any one relationship of which we were all part.

Then I remembered I had experienced a similar response in the past when considering Zen koans, though I had not fully appreciated it at the time. Even now, nearly twenty years later, during times of inner turmoil, or quiet reflection, I continue to pursue the original question, "Who are you apart from all relationships?"

Gradually a satisfying answer has emerged. It is a wordless answer, so I cannot describe it in linear terms, but it is a sense of knowing which I associate with God, and it is extremely comforting. It is characterised by a physical sense of centredness in my body, and deep, even breathing. I still struggle to keep this answer in mind when I most need to remember it – at times of conflict in my marriage or at times of self-doubt.

At this point, I have been married nearly fifteen years to my husband, Charlie Johnson. I feel a deep sense of appreciation and gratitude for the gift of this continuing relationship. However, life has taught me that there are no guarantees. Fate or death may someday rob me of my husband. Because I have become more differentiated, rather than spending my time fearing such things, this awareness allows me to more fully appreciate the relationship we share.

I invite you now to pause and take a moment to experience your own answer to the question of self.

One Small Step

Set aside half an hour in a quiet place. Find a comfortable position, and allow your breathing to develop an even, soothing rhythm. Then gently ask yourself "Who you are apart from all relationships?"

   Don't worry about finding the "right" answer, or even finding a satisfying answer immediately. Simply asking the question is valuable because it allows you to start experiencing the internal state in yourself which will eventually become your answer. Repeat this question at various intervals over the next days, weeks and months, as often as you find meaningful.

Enhancing Differentiation from Your Partner

Another way to enhance your level of differentiation is to approach it on a cognitive, intellectual level. Because some people prefer a more linear approach, I have developed an exercise which can be used on its own or as an adjunct to the "Who are you apart from all relationships?" question.

One Small Step

Allow yourself to focus on each of the following questions separately, progressing only to the level of questions that you feel able to answer at this point. You may complete this exercise in one sitting if you wish, or pursue the questions gradually over the course of days, weeks or months, writing your answers as you determine them.

Beginning Level
1.   In what ways are you similar to your partner?
2.   In what ways are you different from your partner?
3.   Among those personality traits you have in common with your partner, which do you most value or like? List them.
4.   Among those personality traits you have in common with your partner, are there any you dislike or make you uncomfortable? If so, list them.

Intermediate Level
5.   Who are you as a person outside of this relationship? How do you positively express these aspects of yourself in your daily life?
6.   How can you help yourself remain relatively calm and centred

during times when your partner is stressed or upset?

7. What are some healthy and meaningful ways for you to soothe or take care of yourself when you are upset and your partner is unable to help?

Advanced/Mature Level

8. What would you most want to remember about your partner if he were no longer present, or no longer living?

9. What do you most hope your partner would remember about you if you were no longer living?

10. What do you hope the survivor will remember about the relationship when death ends your time together?

Don't be concerned if you have difficulty answering some of these questions. Except for those rare individuals who emerge from a nurturing childhood with a profound sense of self and the resulting ability to soothe themselves regardless of what is going on in their life, differentiation is something that must be earned by rising to the challenges and difficulties that a relationship presents.

And don't worry if you can't immediately access all your newly discovered personal resources when relationship crises occur. Differentiation is a gradual developmental process that most of us continue to pursue (or avoid!) unconsciously or consciously all our lives. The more differentiated we become, the more flexible and resourceful we are in relationships, tolerating, containing and eventually moving beyond the inevitable anxiety that occurs during stressful life events.

YOUR FAMILY OF ORIGIN

In order to become more differentiated in your relationship with your partner, it is first necessary to strengthen your ability to maintain a sense of self that is distinct and independent from your parents and the rest of the family in which you grew up. The next exercise will help you strengthen this ability.

Enhancing Differentiation from Your Family of Origin

One Small Step

Allow yourself to focus on each of the following questions separately, progressing to the level of questions that you feel able to answer at this point. You may complete this exercise in one sitting if you wish, or pursue the questions gradually over the

course of days, weeks or months, writing your answers as you
determine them.

Beginning Level
1.   In what ways are you similar to each of your parents?
2.   In what ways are you different from each of them?
3.   Among those personality traits or characteristics you most
     have in common, which do you most value or like? What is the
     most satisfying and healthy way for you to express this in
     everyday life?
4.   Among the personality traits or characteristics that you have in
     common with each parent, which are the ones you least value?
     What is the most healthy and productive way for you to
     manage or express or transform these characteristics?

Intermediate Level
5.   Who are you as a person, apart from your relationship with
     your parents? How do you, or could you, most positively
     express these aspects of yourself in your daily life?
6.   How can you help yourself remain relatively calm and centred
     during times when one of both of your parents are stressed or
     upset?
7.   What are some healthy and meaningful ways for you to soothe
     or take care of yourself when you are upset and your parents
     are unable to help?

Advanced/Mature Level
8.   What do you want to remember about your parents when they
     are no longer living?
9.   What do you hope your parents would remember about you if
     you were no longer living?

This exercise can also be used with siblings, extended family and
friends.

As with the questions for Enhancing Differentiation from Partner
exercise, don't worry if you don't find all of the questions easy to answer.
However, if any of the questions evoke severe anxiety, consider whether
you might benefit from pursuing them with the support of a
psychotherapist.

Moving Beyond Old Issues with a Parent
As an adult, Daniel was still hampered by anger towards his parents. He
told me, "I wasted a lot of time blaming my parents for the fact that I

wasn't living the kind of life I wanted. Not that some blame wasn't warranted. They made a lot of mistakes in the way they raised me, some of them real bad ones. My father used to beat me, and my mother criticised me all the time and never noticed anything I did right. But spending my time blaming them after I became an adult took up energy that I needed in order to make a good life for myself."

Unfortunately, reclaiming the energy we spend continuing to blame our parents is easier said than done, especially when the resentment stems from childhood abuse. If unresolved feelings about your parents are interfering with your ability to focus on creating a good life for yourself, the following two exercises will help.

 One Small Step
Allow at least half an hour to complete this exercise.
Find a comfortable position and allow an image of your parent to form in your mind. You will need three pieces of paper and a pen.

1. On the first piece of paper, list everything you resent about your parent.
2. On a separate piece of paper, list everything you appreciate about your parent. Remember to include anything you learned from your parent.
3. Based on your first two lists, write on a third piece of paper those aspects you appreciate and would like continue to influence your current life or your current relationship with your parent.
4. Now burn pages 1 and 2, and reread page 3.

Strengthening Your Relationship with Your Parents
This next exercise can be done immediately after completing the previous one, or at a later time when you wish to focus on the positive aspects of your relationship with your parents.

 One Small Step
Allow at least half an hour to complete this exercise. Find a comfortable position and allow an image of your parents to form in your mind. You will need paper and a pen.

1. Record those aspects of the time you currently spend with your parents that you want to remember when you are their age. (If your parents are no longer living and you are experiencing unresolved feelings of hurt or resentment towards them,

substitute the Healing Letters exercise in the next chapter.)

2. Now list what you most hope they would remember about this same time.

3. Write down the aspects of the relationship that you would like to continue.

4. If you have had recent conflicts with your parents, write down what is different about the times when there has been less conflict or things have been more comfortable between you. How might you contribute to making such times occur more frequently?

The above two exercises can be used to address unresolved feelings towards siblings, extended family and other important people from your past.

When Parents Continue to Be Hurtful

If you find yourself feeling overwhelmed and anxious when you are with your parents, try using the following technique.

 One Small Step

Imagine that twenty or thirty years have passed and your parents are no longer alive. How would you wish to have spent the times when you were with them during those intervening years?

Judy had long ago given up focusing on the pain she had endured while growing up with alcoholic and abusive parents. She had devoted her energy first to a successful career as a teacher, later to her marriage and then to providing a nurturing environment for her five-year-old son.

She loved her teaching job, was happy in her marriage and felt delight in watching her young son grow and discover the world around him. Judy considered herself fortunate. The painful childhood she had endured made her present contentment and joy all the more precious.

Several times a year, during the Thanksgiving, Christmas and Easter holidays, Judy and her small family journeyed across the country to visit her aging parents. She dreaded these visits, but continued with them out of a sense of duty. "After all," she told herself, "they are my parents. I owe them this." Her husband did not enjoy these visits, but he respected Judy's need to spend time with her family. His own parents had died earlier in his adult life.

On each visit, Judy's father would belittle Judy and her husband's professional and educational accomplishments. Her mother constantly criticised Judy's choice of clothing and the way she was raising her son. When Judy pointed out to her parents that their belittling and criticising behaviour was hurtful, they ridiculed her as being overly sensitive and unable to accept the "truth" about herself.

Throughout the visits, her mother would reminisce about Judy's childhood, talking about all the wonderful times she remembered. Her father's beatings and her mother's alcoholic lapses and verbal abuse were deleted from these idealised descriptions. When Judy would gently remind her mother that there had been some difficult times also, her mother would angrily tell Judy what a pitiful, ungrateful excuse for a daughter she was.

As each holiday approached, Judy would become increasingly depressed. She became irritable with her husband and son, and impatient with her students. She began to wake in the middle of the night asking herself, "Why am I doing this?" The answer was, "Because I feel I have no choice but to go on visiting my parents. And I don't want to go."

Finally, alarmed by suicidal feelings, Judy visited a psychotherapist. She did not want to kill herself, but she had reached the point at which she could not face another painful visit with her parents. The therapist suggested counselling which would include Judy and her parents. When Judy proposed this to her parents, they angrily refused.

The therapist observed to Judy, "You can't control what they do, but you can control what you do. When you are an old woman and they are no longer alive, how do you imagine you will want to have spent these next twenty years?"

In response to that question, Judy decided that as an old woman, she would want to remember happy holidays in her own home with her husband and son and their friends. As a result she decided to limit visits to her parents to twice a year. She would send them loving cards and letters on the holidays, but she would no longer expose herself and her family to their emotional battering at the times of the year when she most wanted to enjoy herself.

Judy also decided to limit the duration of visits with her parents to two days. This was the amount of time that she could handle without becoming seriously depressed. Since interactions with her parents seemed to go better when there were planned activities, she arranged to visit museums and attend movies while visiting them and invited them to accompany her if they chose.

A few years after making these decisions, Judy told me, "I feel I have worked things out with my parents as well as I can. When I was growing up they did some kind and good things for me as well as the abusive things. I love them because they are my parents. But I will not allow them to make me miserable and even suicidal as an adult. My responsibility these days is to my own family: my husband, my child and myself."

As a child, any attempt to limit the pain her parents caused her had only brought Judy more abuse. While living under her parents' roof, Judy had no choice but to comply with their demands and to accept their abusive behaviour. As an adult, however, she had the power to decide how and when she wanted to interact with her parents.

If your parents behave hurtfully towards you at this point in your life, letting them know that you find certain behaviours painful may result in them changing. If not, you might propose family counselling, or, like Judy, you might choose to alter the way you spend time with them.

Your Children

The following exercise will help you apply the principles and ideas from the earlier sections of this chapter to your relationships with your children. If you have children or you are a caregiver for a child, take a moment now to answer the following questions.

One Small Step
Allow at least half an hour to complete this exercise. Find a comfortable position and allow an image of your child to form in your mind.

1. What do you most appreciate about your child? What aspects of your relationship do you most want to continue?
2. If you have conflicts or problems with your child, what was different about the times when there was less conflict or things were more comfortable? How might you arrange to have these times occur more frequently?
3. When your children are the age you are now, what do you want them to look back on and remember about this time in your relationship?

Again, I recommend recording your answers to the questions. You can review them whenever you want to remember what is special about your child. And undoubtedly, if you repeat the exercise at distant intervals, your answers will be a history of the growth of your relationship.

The exercises in the next section will help you identify and control the effects that painful past experiences may be having on your relationship with your children, partner or other important people in your life.

THE EFFECT OF PAST PAIN
ON CURRENT RELATIONSHIPS

Have you ever felt that you are placing more importance on a casual relationship or a minor aspect of a more important relationship than it warrants? One of the legacies of trauma and abuse which can especially affect relationships is the tendency to fluctuate between idealised and overly critical views of yourself and other people, and to under-emphasise or over-emphasise certain characteristics in order to justify these views. The result is often a phenomenon called "transference".

What is transference? In the Woody Allen movie, *Annie Hall*, there is a scene in which two lovers are in bed together seemingly sharing an intimate moment. However, they are not alone. Images of each of their respective family members and ex-lovers are superimposed on the scene.

In this way, the cinematographer humorously depicts the excess emotional baggage each of them brings to their relationship through transference. Transference refers to unconsciously ascribing or "transferring" feelings and assumptions you had about one significant person in your life to someone else.

The person to whom you direct these feelings usually bears some resemblance to the person who originally evoked them. However, at least some of the beliefs and feelings that you associate with the new person are likely to be inaccurate. Transference can prevent us from perceiving and appreciating the unique qualities of our loved ones. Transference can also render us vulnerable to disappointment and exploitation.

For example, if you had a loving relationship with an immigrant grandfather, transference might cause you automatically to feel kindly towards other paternalistic males with foreign accents before taking into account their actual character traits. I once met a sociopathic building contractor who had swindled many people. When I hired him I didn't know this history. Something about the "goodness" I imagined I perceived in him prevented me from checking his credentials.

Later, I realised the "goodness," I thought I had seen in him was really my re-experiencing feelings I had in childhood with my great-grandfather who spoke with a soft French accent and had beautiful white hair. Because of the similarity of having a foreign accent and white hair, I had unconsciously "transferred" these warm pleasant feelings to the contractor without assessing their accuracy.

When I subsequently learned of the corrupt and exploitative things the contractor had done to many other clients, I felt angry and betrayed.

When I realised how different the contractor actually was from my great-grandfather, the transference was undone. I realised that he showed no integrity in his business dealings, and had only a superficial resemblance to the relative I had loved. Thankfully, this realisation allowed me to prevent the contractor from further exploiting me financially.

While I transferred positive feelings to a person who did not merit them, transference can also cause you to experience unjustified negative feelings towards people. When a person exhibits a personality trait, physical appearance or gesture, or creates a situation that subconsciously reminds you of a painful past experience, the resulting transference can tarnish your feelings towards them even though they have done nothing to deserve it.

This phenomenon is especially tragic and damaging when parents transfer or "project" negative feelings from the past onto their innocent and vulnerable young children. Learning to identify and take responsibility for your own transference will help prevent you causing pain to your own children and other people.

The following exercise will help you identify, control and eventually undo the effects of your own transference in your current relationships. Your responses to people in the future will be based on accurate information about them rather than on old feelings about someone from the past.

 One Small Step

Set aside thirty minutes to write your answers to the questions. Think of someone with whom you are repeatedly upset.

1. Does this person remind you of someone significant from your past? Does some aspect of your relationship with this person remind you of any experience in your past that elicited similar emotions?
2. If you answered Yes to either of the above questions, make a list of how the person or situation in the present is similar to the person or situation from the past. Do these similarities provide any clues as to how you might best deal with the present situation?
3. Now list how the present person or situation differs from the past person or situation.
4. Based on these differences, how might you most fairly and effectively deal with the present person? Now you can begin to adjust your behaviour towards them.

Over-idealisation

By over-idealising other people you set yourself up for disappointment. No one is perfect, and close examination of oneself or another person usually reveals this rather quickly. People who seem "too good to be true" may in fact be exactly that.

Realising belatedly that a friend is not as perfect as you once thought can result in feelings of betrayal. Therefore, it is important to understand the difference between being disappointed by someone's failure to live up to your expectations and actually being betrayed by someone. If your feelings result solely from someone's inability to live up to idealised assumptions about them, remind yourself that your expectations of perfection were unrealistic. Realising this and acting accordingly can prevent you from unfairly alienating the other person and prematurely ending a potentially rewarding friendship.

One Small Step

Think of someone with whom you are repeatedly upset. Take a moment to examine whether your feelings are the result of an unrealistic expectation about that person.

Possibilities

How might you adjust your expectations to more accurately reflect what you know to be true of that person?

What, if anything, do you want or hope for in this relationship?

Abusive and Exploitative People

Another problem with idealising people is that you can become vulnerable to unscrupulous individuals who want to take advantage of you. An example is a corrupt business person who first develops and then exploits customers' trust in order to financially defraud them.

Some people are also emotional exploiters. They may initially present themselves as trustworthy and caring. The purpose of friendships or relationships is solely to benefit themselves. They often reveal themselves as emotional exploiters by being extremely selfish.

For instance, when an emotional exploiter is not in control of a situation - when they do not feel superior, or when you do not give them their own way - they are likely to become angry. They may become verbally abusive in an attempt to bully you into giving them their way, or they may threaten to end the relationship in an attempt to manipulate you.

They especially prey on people who idealise them because such illusions make their victims gullible and overly trusting. If you encounter an abusive or exploitative person in your life, and chances are you will at some time or another, it is important to set limits with them and stand up for yourself. Recognise their anger for what it is: an attempt to manipulate you into complying with their demands.

The Trap of Cynicism

If you have been exploited or abused in a past relationship, you may become distrustful and cynical and close yourself off from new relationships. This is tragic and it plants the seeds of bitterness and loneliness. One way to protect yourself from the trap of cynicism is to allow yourself to trust people gradually and to avoid placing yourself in vulnerable situations with people that you don't yet know well. The following two questions can help you read the safety level of situations requiring your trust.

 Possibilities

How well do I really know this person?

How do I objectively know that what he or she is saying is true?

This chapter has offered a variety of strategies for overcoming the effects of past trauma and other painful life experiences on your current relationships. However, the final legacy of improving your ability to have relationships extends far beyond overcoming the negative effects of your past. You are making room for continuing and heartfelt relationships with many joyous experiences.

The next chapter will help you prevent past experiences from detracting from the quality of your life and your relationships, now and in years to come.

Chapter Eight
Coping When the Past Rears its Ugly Head

> The Buddha said, "A man walking along a high road
> sees a great river, its near bank dangerous and
> frightening, its far bank safe. He collects sticks and
> foliage, makes a raft, paddles across the river, and
> reaches the other shore. Now suppose that, after he
> reaches the other shore he takes the raft and puts it on
> his head and walks with it on his head wherever
> he goes ..."
>
> – Stephen Mitchell

Like the raft, painful past experiences can become an emotional weight that you carry around with you, a burden that interferes with your ability to move freely and enjoy your life. This chapter will help you free yourself of unwanted baggage from the past, while reaping the benefits of the strengths and skills you acquired as a result of coping with painful experiences. The first section will teach you how to unload intrusive images left over from past traumas. The second section addresses unresolved issues with past relationships. And the final section helps you take advantage of what you have learned from the traumatic episodes in your life. The exercises in this chapter will free a significant amount of your energy.

Flashbacks

Sometimes traumatic or painful experiences from the past show up in the form of *flashbacks*, moments comprised of intrusive thoughts and images.

Besides being unpleasant and upsetting these incidents can interfere with your concentration and ability to participate fully in the current moment.

Coming into contact with people or situations that directly or indirectly remind you of unpleasant past experiences can trigger flashbacks. Seemingly unrelated experiences in the present can also trigger a flashback if something about the experience evokes feelings of vulnerability or anxiety that are similar to those you experienced in the past.

Have you ever suffered from unpleasant intrusive thoughts or images? Most people have at one time or another. For example, if you were in a car accident or had a near collision one afternoon on your way home from work, you may have found that later in the evening as you began to relax or tried to sleep, images of the other car or sounds of squealing tires intruded into your consciousness.

Some people suffer recurrent intrusive thoughts or images. Others experience them infrequently, usually after a similarly traumatic event resurrects memories from the past.

I met Claire the day after she had witnessed her partner being robbed at gunpoint outside their car. Although neither had been physically harmed, the experience had been extremely frightening for both of them and resulted in upsetting and unwelcome images typical of post-traumatic stress.

A few hours after the robbery, as they tried to relax in the safety of their home, Claire and her partner found themselves involuntarily reliving the experience with the robber. Images of the robber's masked face and his outstretched arm with the gun kept returning, along with accompanying feelings of terror as they wondered, "Is he going to kill us? What is he going to do to us after he gets the money?"

As is often the case with post-traumatic stress, the intrusive thoughts and images continue on into the night and reoccur the next day. After she described what had happened to her, I taught Claire the Write, Read and Burn technique. It proved effective for Claire and for her partner, whom she taught it to later that evening.

Write, Read and Burn

Because of its simplicity and brevity, the Write, Read and Burn exercise is typically the first intervention I suggest to people requesting relief from intrusive thoughts and traumatic images. Developed at the Milwaukee Brief Family Therapy Center, this technique provides fairly rapid relief for most people.

 One Small Step
You will need paper, pen and a lighter or matches.

1. Write a description of the intrusive image(s) or thought(s).
2. Read it aloud to a supportive person, or if no one is available read it aloud to yourself while imagining the support of a person you know would be a compassionate listener.
3. Now take the paper on which you wrote the description of the intrusive thoughts or images, tear it up, and burn it.

Reading the description aloud and then burning the paper interrupts the pattern of intrusive thoughts by symbolically providing a new ending and resolution to the traumatic event.

The Read, Write and Burn exercise alone may provide full relief, but you might want to repeat it when intrusive thoughts or images reoccur or when new ones arise. Others find this exercise works best when followed by the Drawing Relief exercise, the Re-Writing Old Messages exercise, and/or the Healing Letters exercise in the next sections of this chapter.

Drawing Relief

You may especially like the Drawing Relief exercise if you like to draw or paint, and you may prefer it to the Write, Read and Burn technique. Although it is an adaptation of a technique originally developed for children (Mills and Crowley, 1986), many adults find the Drawing Relief exercise a satisfying way to interrupt the intrusive flow of negative thoughts or images, and that it provides a healing resolution by creating a new, more affirmative ending. Like the previous exercise, it is not difficult and typically provides fairly rapid relief.

 One Small Step
You will need drawing paper, coloured pencils or crayons, or coloured markers, or paints. Allow at least an hour of free time. You are going to draw or paint three pictures.

1. Draw a picture of the image or feelings you associate with the intrusive thought. Use whatever colours best evoke this for you. Don't worry about how you choose to represent this artistically. You may draw a literal image or create an abstract representation of lines, shapes and colours. However you express it is the right way because it is your way.
2. On a separate piece of paper, draw a second picture depicting the absence of the intrusive image. This represents what you would prefer to be feeling or thinking in place of the unwanted image. Again, don't worry about style, concentrate on expressing your preferred thought or feeling in any way that fits you.

3. On a third piece of paper, draw a new picture symbolising how you imagine you got from the state of mind depicted in the first picture to the state of mind depicted in the second picture
4. Now tear up the first picture.

Linda had been emotionally abused by one of the teachers in her college art department. When she rebuffed his sexual advances, he began attacking her work in class. Rather than providing constructive criticism, he ridiculed her work and humiliated her in front of fellow students.

Through dogged determination, Linda was able to endure her teacher's repeated verbal attacks long enough to pass his class and complete a graduate degree in art. Although the experience had shaken her confidence, she never stopped painting in her free time, and began to regain some of her confidence as colleagues began to recognise and appreciate her work.

But when Linda was eventually invited to display her work in a juried art show, the abuse inflicted by the sadistic teacher reared its ugly head in the form of a painful flashback. Linda found herself vividly remembering the teacher's devastating words, "Your work is frivolous, notable only for its evidence of your singular lack of talent." But the most disturbing aspect of the flashback was the image of the contemptuous expression on her teacher's face. Unbidden, this image kept returning to Linda's mind, unravelling her hard-earned self-confidence.

Because drawing and painting were her favourite means of self-expression, I suggested that Linda try the Drawing Relief exercise as a way of getting rid of the unwanted (and inaccurate!) message she had internalised.

First Linda drew a picture of herself as a young student with the critical teacher standing over her. In this picture he was much larger than her. In her second picture, she drew an image of herself standing in front of an exhibition of her paintings with a serene and happy expression on her face.

In her third picture, the one illustrating how she got from the first picture to the second picture, Linda drew herself surrounded by a circle of supportive and encouraging colleagues and teachers from her past and present. The abusive teacher was depicted standing outside the circle unable to get near Linda. In this picture he was smaller than Linda's other teachers and colleagues and was smaller than the image of Linda herself.

Linda then tore up the first picture and kept the other two, looking at them whenever she felt vulnerable about the approaching art exhibition. Participating in the exhibition was a healing experience for her and a turning point in her career.

Rewriting Old Messages

Inaccurate and unwanted negative messages from parents, caregivers, teachers and other authority figures sometimes inadvertently become a part of our self-image.

If the teacher's negative message about the value of Linda's work (rather than the expression on his face) had been the dominant feature of her traumatic flashback, I would have suggested she try the following exercise, adapted from a technique first created by Lucia Cappachione in the *Creative Diary*.

 One Small Step

Consider a negative or destructive message from your past that interferes with your confidence or your positive feelings about your life. Now think of a new and healthy message you would like to receive instead. Write the new message first with your dominant hand, then with your non-dominant hand, several times until it begins to feel like a familiar part of your belief system.

Using the non-dominant hand as well as the one you normally write with connects the message to your right brain, the hemisphere neurologists believe to be associated with unconscious processes. Assuming you took in a negative message on an unconscious as well as a conscious level, using both hands to write the same message more fully integrates the corrective information.

The impact of this healthy new message can be strengthened by writing it repeatedly. Don't worry if the positive message doesn't feel "real" or accurate the first few times you write it; it will gradually surface in your behaviour and the way you think about yourself and your life.

Marly, a talented pianist, took great joy in her continuing study and mastery of classical pieces. However, whenever her husband or friends asked her to play for them, she became frozen with anxiety, remembering her father's angry words.

Marly was six years old, struggling to learn the simple melody of that week's piano lesson. Her father, a severe alcoholic, was at home that afternoon trying to sleep off a vicious hangover. When he was woken up by the sound of the piano, he became enraged and screamed at the little girl, "You can't even play a simple tune, you idiot! Shut the door. Nobody wants to hear you."

I asked Marly to imagine what message she would like to install to replace the painful one she remembered from the past. After considering this for a few moments, she thought of the words she tells her own daughter as she practices her weekly piano lessons, "You're getting better every time you play, and it makes me so happy to hear you."

Marly wrote out the new message for herself, first with her dominant hand and then with her non-dominant hand, repeating this process at various intervals throughout the next few days until the message began to feel natural and comfortable to her.

Unfinished Relationships

Intrusive thoughts and images may be accompanied by powerful feelings specifically associated with a significant person from your past. Your relationship with that person often feels "unfinished" or somehow incomplete.

In her poignant and humorous book about a daughter coming to terms with conflicting feelings and memories of her mother, *Divine Secrets of the Ya-Ya Sisterhood*, Rebecca Wells describes the effects of powerful emotional memories on a young woman trying to enjoy an evening walk:

> *Although she carried a flashlight, and the light of the moon was strong, if she wasn't careful, the very vividness of her memories would cause her to lose her footing.*

Wells' character had the benefit of family and friends to support her in coming to terms with her emotional baggage from the past. Unfortunately, such support is not always available to us.

Resolving past issues that involve another person can become more complicated if their participation is required. Even if you are ready to seek the relief that comes from actively working to get rid of your emotional baggage, the other people involved may not share your motivation. The person from your past may be unwilling, or unavailable, to work things out with you.

Carla was sexually abused by her grandfather. Though several years had passed, she still struggled with feelings of hurt and anger about the abuse. Understandably, she wanted him to acknowledge what he had done and express remorse for the pain he had caused her. But it was clear that this would never happen. He was in the advanced stages of Alzheimer's disease and could not even recognise family members, much less think responsibly and reasonably about what Carla wished to discuss with him.

In other situations, the person with whom you have past issues may no longer be present in your life, or may no longer be living. When Jason was a teenager, his father died suddenly in an accident. Prior to the accident, Jason and his dad had been struggling with one another. His dad disapproved of Jason's membership in a local street gang. Jason was angry at his dad for divorcing his mum. Now five years later, Jason is aware of many happy as well as painful memories of his dad.

Jason used to waiver between remembering his dad as "all good" or "all bad". Neither view was accurate. Furthermore, he never had the opportunity to make his peace with his dad and to say goodbye. He longs for the sense of closure this would bring.

The person who wronged you may not be willing to try to resolve things with you. Kathy's marriage had ended when her husband Dave suddenly left her and their two pre-school children for a relationship with another woman. He gave her no explanation.

Even years after, he still refused to discuss what had happened. After the divorce, Kathy began to date other men, but when a relationship grew serious, unresolved feelings towards Dave would interfere. Kathy found herself taking out the anger and distrust left over from her marriage on her new partner.

Roberta had unresolved anger towards her stepfather. He had sexually abused her younger sisters and physically abused her mother. Despite the fact that the abuse had been witnessed by several family members, the stepfather still denied it. He was not psychologically available for the women to resolve their issues with him.

The Healing Letters exercise is a powerful method for resolving pain from unfinished relationships like the ones I have just described. Because it is not possible to predict the availability or degree of co-operation from people in your past, the Healing Letters do not rely on their participation to be effective.

The Healing Letters will allow you to move forward psychologically in ways that would not be possible if you had to depend solely on responses from the person who wronged you. When the other person *is* available and willing to work with you to resolve past issues, these letters can serve as a psychological preparation for your real conversations with them.

Completing the Healing Letters exercise will help free you from negative messages or beliefs about what was done to you – inaccurate internalised messages about yourself that you unconsciously and uncritically adopted as a result of abuse or trauma.

Your Healing Letters

Please read all the instructions in this section before beginning the Healing Letters exercise.

The Healing Letters were designed to be written. As an alternative, you can speak them aloud, or compose them in your mind. Typically, however, people achieve the most powerful results from writing them.

Address your letters to the person(s) towards whom you have unresolved feelings. Don't write your letters with the intent of mailing them. (After completing your Healing Letters, you may mail one of them if you wish. However, anticipating the letter's impact while you are writing it could interfere with its therapeutic effect by inhibiting your self-expression.)

The Healing Letters are divided into four parts. Letter 1 can be completed by itself in one sitting. Letters 2 and 3 are to be completed at the same time; Letter 3 must be written *immediately* after Letter 2. This is to ensure that this process is therapeutic rather than traumatic. Letter 4 may be completed at a separate time.

Reserve at least one hour for Letter 1, at least two hours Letters 2 and 3 combined, and at least one hour for Letter 4. Most people complete these letters over three consecutive days, but it is fine to give yourself more time between letters, as long as you do not let time pass between Letters 2 and 3.

The Healing Letters can be repeated as needed to increase your feelings of resolution, and further clear away any burdensome feelings that remain from your past.

One Small Step
Letter 1. Releasing Unresolved Thoughts and Feelings

Address this letter to the person for whom you have unresolved feelings or issues. Describe how knowing this person has affected you, including the impact of their words or actions. Include a statement of what you would like from this person in response to your letter.

The purpose of this letter is for you to articulate and further acknowledge any thoughts or feelings you have about what happened in this past relationship that still hurts you.

One Small Step
Letter 2. Releasing Internalised Negative Messages

Write an imaginary response from the person you wrote to in Letter 1. Reflect any fears you have about what the person might say back to you, as well as any fears you have about their refusing to listen or to try to understand what you communicated in Letter 1. Once written, it is important that you do not dwell on Letter 2, but move *immediately* to Letter 3.

The purpose of the second letter is to get rid of any negative beliefs or messages about yourself that were internalised as a result of what this person did to you.

One Small Step

Letter 3. Releasing Internalised Hopes

Write a different imaginary response from the person that wronged you. Unlike Letter 2, reflect your hopes and wishes about how the other person might respond. Communicate his or her willingness to take responsibility for what they did to you, expressing their remorse in a compassionate response to the resentment you brought up in Letter 1.

The purpose of Letter 3 is to provide the healing resolution that comes with the response you would have liked or once hoped to receive in real life.

One Small Step

Letter 4. Releasing Yourself

Your Response to Letter 3

Write a final letter to the person who hurt you. Respond to what they said in Letter 3, reflecting the changes and resolution it afforded you. Include any final business that you left unsaid in Letter 1 or have thought of since.

You may write this letter immediately after Letter 3, or you can wait several days, weeks or even months.

Remember, no two people will write the same letters even if they are addressing the same wrong-doer. The best indications of your having written successful Healing Letters are your feelings of peace and comfort afterwards.

Healing Letters in Action

Because of old pain and resentment stemming from her stepfather's abuse, it was hard for Roberta to trust her boyfriend, and at times she became inappropriately angry with him. Examining these feelings, she realised that she was transferring unresolved feelings about her stepfather onto her current relationship. Writing the Healing Letters allowed Roberta to free herself from this emotional burden and move on to enjoy a good relationship with her boyfriend.

Sample Letter 1. (Roberta wrote to her stepfather describing what he had done, how she felt and what she wanted from him.)

Dear Roger

You sexually abused my little sisters and cousins, and you
physically abused my mother. Over the years I kept hoping you
would choose to tell the truth and say that you are sorry for what
you did. I am still very angry at you because you hurt them so
badly. It has been very painful for me to see the results of what you
did to them. Not just your molesting them, but the message it sent
them: that their feelings didn't count. Each of them has had trouble
believing in herself and hasn't had the confidence to succeed at
doing what she wants in her life. As a result their lives have been
very hard. They have had trouble holding down jobs and have had
a history of choosing men who batter them, just like you did Mom.

You have always refused to tell the truth, and refused to say
you were sorry even years later when they tried to talk to you. By
continuing to lie, you made it even more difficult for them to move
beyond the effects of your abuse. This makes me feel very angry
and very sad. And seeing the results of what you did to them has
made it hard for me to trust other men in my life, even kind and
good men from my church group, because I have feared that they
would behave like you.

I am writing this because I want you to tell the truth about
what you did. I want you to say you were sorry, so that my sisters
and my mother and I can forgive you. I was going to add to the
previous sentence, "so that we can all move on with our lives."

But the fact is, I have decided I am going to move on with my
life with or without your apology. You are *not* going to ruin my life
in the future.

Sincerely
Roberta

Sample Letter 2. (Roberta imagined and wrote out the following
response from Roger to release any fears or negative messages she may
have internalised and taken in unconsciously.)

Dear Roberta

Not for the first time, I am appalled by your crazy, distorted
perceptions. You are trying to blame your own screw-ups and your
mother's and sisters' failures in life on imagined childhood abuse
at my hands. I never did anything to them or to your cousins. And
I never did anything to hurt your mother. They are lying, just like
you. You are just trying to hurt me and interfere with my
relationship with your mother.

I am glad that I never have to see you again.

Sincerely
Roger

Sample Letter 3. (Roberta wrote the following imaginary response from Roger as a way of releasing her old hopes and longings about what she needed him to say to her in order to provide her with closure and psychological resolution.)

Dear Roberta
I felt deeply sad after reading your letter and realising the terrible effects of what I did. I am deeply sorry for the things I did that hurt your mother and your sisters and cousins and that hurt you. I want you to know that I did not think at the time that what I was doing to your mother and to those little girls would have the awful impact it did on them and on you. I believe if I had thought about that I would not have molested them, and I never would have hit your mother.

I know I can never make up for what I did, but I am trying to help by supporting your sisters and your cousins in paying for their counselling and their efforts to heal. I have told your mother I am sorry. I hope that you and they will find it in your hearts to forgive me. I wish you well. I wish you a good life, one that makes up for the bad things that happened in our family when you were a kid.

Sincerely
Roger

Sample Letter 4. (Roberta responded to Letter 3 to further her resolution and closure.)

Dear Roger
Thank you for your willingness to hear what I had to say, and for your response. It makes a difference for me. My heart feels a little lighter. I wish you God's light and peace on the rest of your life journey.

Sincerely
Roberta

BENEFITTING FROM YOUR PAST

Allen, a 32-year-old teacher, was physically assaulted by two strangers who had beaten him up for no apparent reason. He explained his reason for scheduling a psychotherapy appointment with me: "I've always felt that things happen for a reason, but I can't figure out how I have anything good to show for what those two guys did to me, beating me up in that parking lot. I keep asking myself, 'Why did this happen?'"

I gently suggested to him that sometimes bad things happen to good people for no apparent reason, and that this is one of the mysteries and tragedies of the human condition. While some people find comfort in the idea that bad things can happen to people in a seemingly random fashion, I could tell immediately that this was not a helpful concept for Allen.

While Allen understood what I meant, this viewpoint did not provide the resolution and completion he needed to move on with his life. He said, "Intellectually I know what you're saying is true, but it doesn't work for me emotionally. I need to find or make some useful meaning out of what happened, even if there is no objective way to prove it."

Recognising a River You Have Crossed
Surviving a traumatic experience is like crossing a river: while fending for yourself you develop new skills that can help you in the future. I created the following exercise for people like Allen who want to reap the benefits of identifying and figuring out how to use what they have learned as a result of surviving a painful experience.

 One Small Step
Set aside at least an hour for this exercise. Think of a painful experience you have survived and briefly describe it.

1. What did you learn from surviving this experience?
2. What strengths or talents did you draw on at the time, or develop later, to survive the experience?
3. How can these strengths or talents be used to your best advantage now?

Carla, a successful attorney in her mid-forties was sexually abused as a child by her grandfather. She explained her dilemma to me: "When my grandfather was abusing me I was so hurt and overwhelmed by the experience that it sort of took over who I was. Later in college, my life became a series of survivor group meetings and political activities aimed at educating people and preventing kids from being abused. The work was very meaningful and still is, but I don't want it to continue to be the whole focus of my life. I need another way to get more distance from what happened so I can move on with my life."

Here is Carla's response to the Recognising a River You Have Crossed exercise:

"I guess the hardest thing I ever went through was being sexually abused by Grandpa. It made me feel like a nothing. Sometimes when it was happening I just wanted to die."

1. (What did you learn from surviving this experience?)

"Surviving it, at first while it was going on, meant that I had to find things to take my mind off it. I remember as a kid practicing the cello for hours, anything to get away from the horrible feelings I had when I would think about what Grandpa was doing to me. I couldn't make him stop because he was a very violent man, and I was afraid of how he would retaliate if I told on him."

2. (What strengths or talents did you draw on at the time, or develop later, to survive the experience?)

"I remember seeing the movie *Chorus Line*, and this woman in the movie talking about how much she liked practicing ballet, because there [at the ballet] everything was beautiful and okay. That's how it was for me with the cello, and that was a sort of talent I developed in order to cope. Later, I got stronger, and in groups I learned to express my feelings and how to get angry when I needed to, and how to stand up for myself.

"Being able to stand up for myself and get angry when it is appropriate was especially important because it was something I could never do when I was being abused. It is a strength I developed later, after the abuse, in order to survive the fact that it had happened to me, and to protect myself from other kinds of abuse. Being able to get angry has helped me stop people from trying to abuse me emotionally or financially."

3. (How can these strengths or talents be used to your best advantage now?)

"As far as using these skills [standing up for myself and playing the cello] to my best advantage in my life right now, I think maybe it's time for me to start playing music again. I haven't played the cello for five or six years. I don't even have one anymore, but I still like listening to music. I want to start spending more time with music, listening to some CDs, maybe going to some concerts. I think I might like to learn a new instrument, one that is more portable, maybe the guitar. As far as standing up for myself, I want to become more assertive at work."

If you have not already done so, take a moment to do the Recognising a River You Have Crossed exercise at the beginning of this section.

Harvesting Your Past

This chapter's final exercise will help integrate the work you did in the previous exercises while you further harvest the knowledge and resources you developed in order to survive the past. As with most other exercises in this book, your responses may be written or recorded on tape. You can repeat it as often as you wish.

 One Small Step

Take a few minutes to daydream about your life in the future. Imagine that you are productively using all the knowledge you have gleaned from both the past experiences you would prefer to forget and those you want to remember.

Everything you have learned is part of your personal wisdom. You don't have to grow old to acquire wisdom, but you do need to live truly and fully.

While this chapter has focused on ways to address and resolve the lingering effects of the past, the next chapter will offer help for coping and finding comfort on those stressful days and nights that sometimes occur in your present life.

Chapter Nine

Dealing with Rainy Days and Dark Nights

... This morning I woke at four and lay awake for an
hour or so in a bad state. It is raining again. I got up
finally and went about the daily chores, waiting for the
sense of doom to lift —and what did it was watering
the house plants. Suddenly joy came back because I
was fulfilling a simple need, a living one.

– May Sarton

Sometimes I found that in my happy moments I could
not believe that I had ever been miserable... While in
my moments of despair I could not even remember
what happiness felt like.

– Joanna Field

Is there anyone in the world who has reached adulthood and never had an
emotionally dark period, the sort we euphemistically refer to as *rainy days*
and *dark nights*? I doubt it.

I have been no stranger to dark days. Divorce, illnesses, deaths of
people I love, and other losses have all triggered rainy days. This chapter
offers a variety of methods for coping with your dark nights and rainy
days, as well as ways to prepare for future gloomy moments.

Rainy days and dark nights are less troubling if you think of them as
transitory rather than permanent states, and remember that they gradually
pass as you go about the business of daily life. Experiencing contrasting
emotional states from day to day is part of living life fully and truly.

I want to emphasise that the emotional states I am talking about in this chapter are not episodes of severe clinical depression. While rainy days or dark nights may evoke uncomfortable feelings of restlessness, anger, confusion, sadness, or anxiety, they are by definition not life threatening. If at any time you experience numerous consecutive days of depression without relief, or if you experience suicidal thoughts, seek professional help.

Taking Care of Yourself

As a psychotherapist I've found that most people forget about the basics when they are upset and need them most. So to begin at the beginning, maintaining your physical health is an important aspect of maintaining your emotional well-being.

Eat a Decent Meal
When you have a bad day or difficult night, check to make sure that you have eaten. Many people forget to eat or eat poorly when they are upset. If you have a tendency towards hypoglycemia (low blood sugar), the lack of food in your system will worsen feelings of depression and anxiety.

Loading up on caffeine and sugar rather than healthy food can also contribute negatively to the intensity of your feelings. This is also true of alcohol. So make sure that your strategy for coping with a difficult time includes a healthy meal or snack.

Get Some Rest
How much sleep have you had? Exhaustion may be contributing to your gloomy period. Like food, sleep (or lack of it) effects the intensity of emotions, particularly negative ones. If you don't believe me, remember the cranky small child who missed his nap.

Sleep deprivation also affects adults. Having struggled with workaholic tendencies, I used to mistake my own state of exhaustion for depression. Eventually I realised that what I thought was a bad day, was usually a day when I was trying to do too much in too short a time, when I had slept too little the night before.

Take a Bath
There is an anonymous saying that was popular in our grandparents' era: "There are few problems that cannot be improved by a hot bath and a good night's sleep." It's still true today.

Take a Break

Remember the Ultradian Rhythms I talked about in Chapter Six? We function best if we take a break every hour and a half to two hours. Ignoring your body's need for these breaks can result in increased stress, difficulty concentrating and a higher risk of illness. Take a twenty-minute break and notice the difference it makes.

Exercise

Do you feel sluggish? Is your body tense? How much exercise have you been getting? A brisk walk or an aerobic workout does a lot more than just tone your body. It will clear your mind, calm your thoughts and you'll sleep better tonight as a result. Exercise also stimulates the production of endorphins, the body's natural anti-depressant.

If you feel that you don't have enough time to exercise regularly, you are probably experiencing a stress level that makes it imperative that you do so! So shelve your other obligations for an hour and get some exercise. You'll get more done afterwards because of your increased energy.

Get a Massage

Are your neck and shoulders tight? Is your stomach churning? Have you been under pressure at home, at work or in general? If so, your body is probably talking to you, maybe even yelling at you in an attempt to get your attention so you'll slow down and relax. Set up an appointment for a massage, you deserve one.

Give Yourself a Foot Rub

Massage your own feet and notice the resulting feelings of relaxation and well-being as you knead, rub and soothe those hard-working muscles. Begin by soaking your feet in a tub of warm salt water, dry them and rub in a peppermint-scented foot lotion. Then work progressively over the upper and lower surface of each foot, using small circular movements.

Get a Medical Check-up

Are you experiencing physical distress? Has it been going on for a while? If your blues are accompanied by consistent physical symptoms, there may be a medical cause. I once found myself in a state of anxiety and frustration because I couldn't seem to carry out my normal obligations and routines, even though I was eating right and getting enough sleep. It was only when I visited my doctor for my yearly checkup that I found out I had mononucleosis, a virus associated with fatigue.

LISTEN TO YOURSELF

Rainy days and dark nights sometimes provide the gift of reassessing your values and beliefs. Sometimes the best way to receive this gift is to acknowledge what you are feeling and listen to your soul's response. Writing about what you are experiencing is a good way to do this. Expressing your feelings in writing can provide release and enough psychological distance to accurately assess the circumstances, event or situation that brought forth the feelings. What are you trying to tell yourself?

As a survivor of sexual abuse, I had a dark night of despair several years ago when the price of my telling the truth resulted in rejection and estrangement from certain people who wanted to protect the abusers at any price. This excerpt from my journal at the time illustrates how the discouraging experience also contained the seed for moving beyond the darkness:

"With great sadness last night, I heard their words, "You are losing your relationship with us [by refusing to lie for us]." I was very disappointed in their lack of integrity in asking me to lie, but I was even more heartbroken by the fact that I had lost my own illusion of goodness about them. In a sense I had lost the people I thought they were, and that loss was irretrievable."

After I had sat crying for a while, a thought came to me, and it is one that I don't ever want to forget, "Yes, you have lost them, but you get to be true to yourself for the rest of your life." I realised that while it can be terrible to lose someone you love, it is worse to lose your integrity. I immediately felt a sense of calm, the seed of which became joy a few hours later when I looked out the window and saw the moonlight shining on the old apple trees.

Remembering Other Rainy Days
What gift have you received from past rainy days and dark nights? Sit quietly and answer the following questions.

One Small Step
Think back to rainy days or dark nights in your past.

Possibilities
What were they like?
What triggered them?
What helped you out of them?
How might you apply this to a current situation in your life right now?

A Personal Ritual
If your dark night or rainy day is characterised by intrusive and upsetting thoughts or images from the past, try the Write, Read and Burn, Drawing Relief or Rewriting Old Messages exercises in Chapter Eight.

Declare a "Snow Day"
How long has it been since you had any time to yourself, away from the outside world? In Northern Michigan, where I grew up, winter was a long season. Fortunately, the snowy, cloud-filled skies brought the gift of "snow days", unplanned holidays that came when the snow was too deep to leave the house. On these days you could do whatever you wanted - catching up on chores or just enjoying yourself around the house. After spending too much time in large crowds, a snow day may be just what you need.

Get out of the House
Did you cringe when I suggested the snow day? Maybe staying indoors is just more of what you have already been doing and is the last thing you need when you have the blues. If so, get outdoors or go somewhere different to your usual environment.
    If the weather is bad, consider indoor botanical gardens, museums or galleries.

Don't Just Sit there, Pound a Pillow!
No, I'm not kidding. Are you angry about something? Sometimes depression or anxiety are the result of anger turned inward. Anger is energy, and discharging it can make you feel better. If pounding a pillow feels too ridiculous, start by expressing your negative feelings in writing and then consider doing some form of physical work as a release.
    Leaf-raking, snow-shoveling, digging a flower bed are all good physical releases. So are scrubbing floors and washing windows, or sanding the paint off an old piece of furniture. Any activity requiring a lot of elbow grease can expel some of your anger. Afterwards you'll feel better, and you'll have accomplished something worthwhile.

Call a Friend
Melancholy thrives on isolation, so does full-blown depression. Ironically, sometimes we choose to be alone when it is the last thing we need. There are two kinds of support a friend can lend when you're feeling down. The first is listening to your troubles, the second is getting your mind off them by talking about other things.

Reconnect to Your Hopes and Dreams

Have you forgotten your cherished hopes and daydreams, or perhaps they seem far away right now? If so, why not take some time to do the Letter from the Future exercise in Chapter Four?

Reconnect to the Present

If your dark night or rainy day is connected to feelings about the past, you may need to mentally reconnect to the present, so you can assess and deal with your feelings with the resources of an adult perspective.

 One Small Step

Take a moment to think about what you reminds you of who you are now. What is different about your environment from where you lived in the past? Take a look around you and note the colours, shapes, sounds and textures.

Imagine the advice you would give to another person who came to you with a problem like yours.

Make Your Favourite Comfort Food

Did you have a favourite food as a child? Mine was plain old macaroni with homemade tomato sauce. These days I gussy it up a little with basil and garlic and a sprinkling of freshly grated Parmesan cheese, and it still brings feelings of well-being. What foods bring comfort to you? Indulged in moderation, they will do no harm, and just may help you feel better.

Plan a Vacation

Sometimes escapism is just what is needed, even if you can't go on a vacation immediately. Instead, spend a few minutes imagining your planned vacation – where would you go? What would you do? Imagine the joy and relaxation you would feel.

Give Yourself a Spa Day

Many health clubs and beauty salons offer day spas during which you can bask during a combination of beauty treatments and a relaxing massage. If you can't afford it, give yourself a treatment at home.

Learn Something New

When was the last time you did something just for the fun of it? Is it time to start a new hobby or develop a new interest? Language classes, crafts and taking up a new sport are just a few of the ways you can bring new life and spark to your life.

Pray

A friend told me about a wonderful saying she learned in Alcoholics Anonymous, "Let go, and let God." Telling God about whatever is troubling you and turning it over to Him or Her, or whoever you imagine God to be, can make a big difference. When I am troubled, regardless of whether I am in my hometown or far away in a foreign country, I go into a church, light a candle and pray. It always helps me.

Help Someone Less Fortunate Than Yourself

After my grandmother died several years ago following a long illness, I found myself feeling emotionally depleted. The world around me seemed bleak without her presence, and my normal grief process seemed in danger of disintegrating into a narcissistic self-pity. I began volunteering at a shelter for homeless women and my perspective quickly shifted.

The possibilities for volunteer work are unlimited. There are Big Sisters, Big Brothers organisations which help disadvantaged youths, homeless shelters, Meals on Wheels, the Red Cross and many more. Helping doesn't need to be limited to other humans. If you are an animal lover, why not volunteer at the local Humane Society, or better yet, adopt a homeless pet. All of our pets were originally strays, and I know from experience that they will return the love and care you give them with undying loyalty and affection.

Perhaps you don't need to look as far as charitable organisations to find an outlet for your desire to help. Is there a friend, a relative, or a neighbour near you who could benefit from your support and kindness? Don't overlook the needs of adolescents and children; along with the elderly they are among our most vulnerable citizens.

CLEARING AWAY
YOUR OUTDATED EXPECTATIONS

Sometimes rainy days occur because you're mistakenly trying to be the person you were in the past, but no longer are. When I was younger and had more time and knew fewer people, I made all my own Christmas presents and baked homemade treats to give to everyone I cared about. The Christmas season was always a joyous time for me.

Then a few years ago I found myself collapsed in bed with the flu in mid-December as I frantically tried to figure out how I was going to bake all those cookies and finish all those half-completed gifts for family and friends.

The fact was, I couldn't. In fact I had probably become sick as a result of trying to produce all those homespun, homemade, heartfelt gifts and treats while shouldering a heavy workload in my professional life. Once I realised that I was no longer the free spirit I had once been before my workload and relationships became extensive, my holidays became serene again. I still give people homemade treats, but oftentimes I purchase them at the local Church bazaar. And I'm able to enjoy the holidays again.

Take a moment now to review your current expectations of yourself. Do they need to be updated to reflect the realities of the life you now live? Are you trying to keep your home as clean as you did when you had fewer responsibilities or you were the only one living in it? If so, maybe you need to re-evaluate your standards, or enlist the help of other people who live there. Or if you can afford it, why not hire a cleaning service? If you are trying to do too much in other areas of your life, consider re-ordering your priorities.

Figure out who You Are apart from Your "Shoulds"
Spending our time doing what we believe we "should" be doing can be not only unsatisfying, but can also deprive us of the joy we deserve from life.

 One Small Step
If left unfettered, but nurtured and supported, how would you choose to pass your time? Notice what thoughts and images come to mind as you imagine this.

 Possibilities
If you lived more in accord with your envisioned preferences rather than spending so much time on what you "should" do, what productive or useful things might occur in your life?
What would be one small step you could take to initiate some of these newly discovered activities?
What small sign would show that you had begun to move in this direction?

Mend an Emotional Fence
Are you holding a grudge against someone you really care about? Is it eating at you? My great-grandmother, who was deservedly famous for her Irish temper, got mad at a close friend over a minor slight. Although the friend lived just down the street, they didn't speak to each other for the next twenty years.

Finally, bursting with a piece of irresistible news (her daughter had given birth to twins) my great-grandmother broke the ice and spoke to her friend. They immediately resumed their relationship as if nothing had happened. In the meantime they had missed out on twenty years of good times they could have shared. My great-grandmother must have felt sad every time she walked past her estranged friend's house.

Consider reaching out to an estranged friend. Or, if you are feeling the pain of a deep emotional wound in a significant relationship, do the Healing Letters exercise in Chapter Eight.

Life is too short to carry the heavy burden of extended suffering from painful past relationships.

Check Your Personal Boundaries
Are you overwhelmed by duties or responsibilities that should not rightfully by yours? Is someone exploiting you by making unreasonable demands on your time and energy? If so, the dark night or rainy day you are experiencing may be an indication that it's time to set limits with that person, to draw a boundary around your availability to them.

With the exception of dependent children and adults unable to care for themselves, each person is responsible for themselves. Consistently doing for others what they need to do for themselves, or repeatedly rescuing them from the consequences of irresponsibility, will accomplish little other than wearing you out. And it can prevent them from taking the necessary actions to move forward in their lives.

 Possibilities
Are other people's expectations infringing on your life?
If so, what is one small change you could make to modify this situation?

Re-organise Your House
I have noticed an interesting phenomenon over the years, especially among women. After re-organising their homes, people often realise in retrospect that they were they were simultaneously re-organising their mental priorities and shifting their psychological perspectives. When you have the time, rearrange the areas in your home to suit your current lifestyle.

 Possibilities
What did you discover about the changes in your life when you re-organised your home?

Preparing for
Future Rainy Days and Dark Nights

While we can't always predict a difficult day or night in advance, creating the Rainy Day Comfort Box and the Rainy Day Letter can help us prepare for difficult times and make their occurrence less upsetting.

The Rainy Day Comfort Box

In *Simple Abundance*, Saran Ban Breathnach suggests outfitting a "comfort drawer" to have ready when you need it. Opening a Rainy Day Comfort Box on a gloomy day and visiting your fondest keepsakes can restore light and beauty to your day.

What nourishes your mind and spirit? Books on aromatherapy offer suggestions for scents that help to induce relaxation, re-invigorate, or invite sleep. Some companies offer herbal bath products labelled according to their aromatic effects.

You might include a favourite book of poems, special letters, cards or photographs that evoke happy memories, a collection of cartoons and jokes you've clipped out of newspapers and magazines. You might also want to include a comforting teddy bear or stuffed animal. You can find many additional ideas in *The Woman's Comfort Book* by Jennifer Louden, a book you may also want to keep in your Rainy Day Comfort Box.

 One Small Step
Line a box or drawer with pretty wrapping paper or cloth in a pattern that delights you. Then put the things you have collected inside.

The Rainy Day Letter

Sometimes you can see a future rainy day approaching on the horizon: a dear friend's terminal illness, the inevitable pain of imminent divorce proceedings, the bittersweet transition of a much-loved child leaving for college. At other times dark nights and rainy days come with no warning. In either case, these difficult times can be eased by preparing for them in advance by creating a Rainy Day Letter.

The Rainy Day Letter is the psychological version of the Rainy Day Comfort Box. Ironically, when we most need comfort is when it's most difficult to remember. The Rainy Day letter will provide personal comfort when you most need it.

Since a letter is more portable, you can carry it with you to support you wherever you are. And it offers the wisdom of the person who knows you best: yourself!

One Small Step
Set aside some time when you are calm and can relate this serenity to yourself at a future time when you are upset, overwhelmed or distressed. Write this letter from you to you.

1. List the activities you find comforting
2. Record the names and phone numbers of supportive friends or family members
3. Remind yourself of your strengths and virtues
4. Remind yourself of your special talents, abilities and interests
5. Remind yourself of some of your hopes and dreams for the future
6. Give yourself special advice or other reminders that are important to you.

Here is part of a Rainy Day Letter I wrote to myself several years ago. It is not intended as an ideal example of how your letter should be, but an illustration to help you start creating your own.

Dear Yvonne
When you read this in the future, you will probably be feeling down on your luck, saddened, weary, upset about something. Whatever you are feeling right now, this letter is for you.

Find a comfortable place to sit down while you read this. Would it help to make yourself a cup of chamomile tea first so you can sip it as you read?

If you are feeling down on yourself right now, I want to remind you that while you are not perfect, you do have some good character traits: you tend to finish what you start, you try hard to be fair and loyal in your relationships and you have a good sense of humour.

Have you eaten? Why not make yourself macaroni with tomato sauce?

Have you been sleeping okay? If not, how about a hot bath and a nap?

What about exercise? Maybe you need to get outdoors. Maybe it would help to take a walk in the woods. Or if you're far from home, why don't you go into to a church and pray? That always helps.

Would it help to call a friend? Maybe you need to talk to Charlie, your husband and best friend of all. Or maybe you need to talk to another woman. You could call ____ or _____ or _____ (phone numbers).

Or maybe you're emotionally drained, worried about something you can't control. If so, why not shut the door and turn off the phone. Watch one of those vintage black-and-white movies from the Forties that you love, or reread your favourite passages from Pablo Neruda's *Odes to Opposites*.

The bottom line here, my dear, is that it's okay, in fact it's important to take some time right now to figure out what you need to do to in order to feel better, and then do it. And remember, what ever it is, this too will pass. Whatever else happens, I will always be here for you, because I am you.

Love,

Me

If you haven't already done so, take some time now to begin your Rainy Day Letter. You deserve the comfort it will bring. Rereading it and implementing some of the ideas in your letter really can make a difference in times of stress and distress. I know this not only from personal experience but from hundreds of people I have seen in my psychotherapy practice and in my workshops.

Finally, remember that nothing, be it a bad day or night or a distressing event, will go on forever. Change is inevitable, and sooner or later this too will pass.

This chapter has offered a variety of things you can do to cope with, learn from, and get past difficult times and prepare for the ones that come in the future. The next chapter will provide suggestions, guidelines and a format for creating the nurturing and exhilarating environment of a Small Steps support group based on the exercises in this book.

PART FOUR

·

SUPPORT AND FURTHER RESOURCES

CHAPTER TEN

HOW TO START A SMALL STEPS SUPPORT GROUP

The only true gift is a portion of yourself.

– Ralph Waldo Emerson

Telling one's troubles to a supportive person undoes the isolation that often worsens pain. You no longer feel alone in trying to cope with your problem.

Similarly, telling another sympathetic person your hopes, dreams and plans strengthens your ability to take action to make these things happen. Talking about a goal can make it feel more real and more achievable. Furthermore, once you have talked to another person about a cherished hope or dream, it is harder to dismiss its importance, forget about it or otherwise lose track of it. A group of supportive people can be invaluable in helping each other identify and then gradually complete the small progressive steps that are part of achieving any goal. Small Steps Groups are designed to provide such mutual aid while fostering each member's continued exploration and creative expression of her Authentic Self.

The first four sections of this chapter provide practical information and guidelines for structuring, starting and ending a Small Steps Support Group. The next section offers basic questions to be used in the group, and the final section is comprised of a collection of exercises that have been adapted for Small Steps Support Groups.

The Group Structure

The organisers should begin by deciding when, where and for how many sessions the group will meet and who will lead the sessions.

You can start a group on your own by inviting several supportive friends, or you can enlist the help of a professional psychotherapist or counsellor to organise and conduct the group. If you enlist the help of a professional make sure that they have been trained in Solution-focused therapy and have had prior experience leading groups.

It is best to start out with a time-limited group, such as four to six sessions, with the provision that at the meeting last group members can elect to continue for another specified period. An initial commitment for longer than six sessions may be daunting for some people and prevent them from joining the group.

Group sessions usually vary from an hour and a half to two hours depending on the size of the group. I suggest that a group have at least three people, but no more than ten. It is imperative that each member gets a chance to talk, and this becomes difficult if a group is too large.

If there is not an official designated leader for the group, members should arrange to rotate leadership among themselves, agreeing in advance how this will be done. The leader is responsible for making sure that each person has a chance to answer the Basic Group Questions, and for selecting one of the group exercises from this chapter.

Setting a kitchen timer is one way to ensure that each member has a chance to speak. I recommend allowing no more than five minutes for each member until everyone has an opportunity to answer the first Basic Group Questions. Some groups will naturally share time more or less equally.

General Guidelines

As a basic ground rule, group members should agree that their role with one another is to be nurturing and validating. The purpose of the group is to provide psychological support and encouragement for people who want to explore their hopes and dreams and actively pursue the series of gradual small steps that will allow them to overcome obstacles and achieve the life they want and deserve.

Criticism or amateur psychoanalysis of one another's shortcomings are *not* a part of the Small Steps Group. Information shared by a member during the meetings is to be kept confidential, and should not be shared or discussed outside the group without that person's permission. The only exception is a situation in which someone is in life-threatening danger.

THE MECHANICS OF A SMALL STEPS SUPPORT GROUP

The first meeting should begin with each member introducing herself and then answering the following questions:

 Possibilities
What would you like to have happen as a result of attending this group?
What are some of the goals, hopes and dreams for which you want support and encouragement from the other group members?
Of these, which goal would you like to begin with?

Whether a Small Steps Group elects to meet for just a few weeks or becomes an ongoing group that meets for months or even years, the Basic Questions are a good way to keep meetings on track and help members acknowledge and support one another's continued growth and progress.

After the first meeting, subsequent meetings are comprised of the Basic Group Questions and completing one exercise listed in the following section. For example, depending on the size of the group, a ninety-minute meeting might be divided into two forty-minute segments with a ten-minute break in between. The first half of the meeting could be devoted to the members answering the Basic Group Questions, then the second half would focus on group members completing and discussing that week's exercise. On occasions when the group undertakes a longer exercise, such as the Time Line or the two-part Creating a New Influence exercise, the members might decide to begin the exercise during their meeting and complete it at home, discussing it in a subsequent meeting.

The final section of this chapter is comprised of written instructions for the Basic Group Questions and the exercises from *Beyond Survival* best suited to a group format. Having spent over three thousand hours leading various groups, I have learned from experience that giving participants individual written instructions simplifies things. For convenience I have listed the questions and exercises on individual pages so they can be photocopied and distributed to group members. Repeatedly using the combination of the Basic Group Questions and the exercises in this chapter will help establish a climate of safety and trust in the group that enables people to identify and enact the small steps that lead to the fulfillment of their hopes and dreams.

ENDING THE GROUP

As the final session of the Small Steps Support Group approaches, invite members to reflect on and tell one another what the group has meant to them and what they have learned from other group members. The Rainy Day Letter from the Group exercise at the end of this chapter can be used when a group is ending or when a member is leaving.

BASIC GROUP QUESTIONS

1. Which aspects of your goal have stayed the same, worsened or improved since that last group meeting?
2. How did the improvements happen?
3. How could you continue the improvements or make them happen more often?

If a group member reports that nothing is better, and is discouraged or disgruntled, they should be invited to answer the following questions:

4. Does the goal you are working on feel too overwhelming or too large? If yes, proceed to question 5. If no, skip question 5.
5. If on a scale of 1 to 10 (10 means that you had achieved the goal, and 1 means that you haven't even thought about wanting to achieve the goal), where are you now? What would raise your score a half a point? What would raise it a whole point? Is this something you want to try? If no or unsure, proceed to the following questions.
6. How is it that things are not worse? What useful things have you or others done to prevent things from getting worse?
7. Is there any advantage, even a small one, to things not getting better for you? If so, how might you manage to preserve some of this advantage while moving forward or improving things?
8. If, after the above questions, a group member is still feeling stuck or discouraged, proceed to the Miracle Question in the next section.

In all cases it is crucial that these questions be offered and received in a supportive, non-critical and respectful spirit, and be based on a sincere desire to help yourself and your fellow group members. If in responding to the Basic Questions, someone becomes sidetracked or has trouble answering, she can ask the group for help and support, or progress to the Miracle Question.

The Miracle Question

Imagine that in the middle of the night, while you were asleep, a miracle happened and you had achieved the hopes, goals or dreams that brought you to this group.

Possibilities
What would be different when you woke up?
What would be the first small change in your behaviour that you would notice?
What would the people who live with you notice?
What would the people you work with notice?
What changes in your behaviour would the other members of the Small Steps Group notice at your next meeting?

One Small Step
Choose one small behavioural change that would represent a step towards your miracle, and practice doing it between now and the next group meeting. Report the results to the group.

If you have trouble coming up with the first small signs that your miracle has happened, try this: imagine that you have a videotape of yourself that started running the moment your miracle happened in the middle of the night. What would you notice yourself doing if you were watching the videotape of yourself the first day (and night) after your miracle had happened? What would be the first image or frame on the videotape that would indicate that your miracle had happened? What would be the next one?

This exercise can be especially useful when you are feeling stuck or dispirited about a problem. It will clarify how your hopes or goals might transpire in real life, and then help you identify the small steps necessary to move towards achieving them.

A Message From A Guardian Angel

Imagine that a wise and compassionate guardian angel has been sitting on your shoulder since you were born. You have not been aware of this presence up until now because angels are weightless. The angel's sole purpose has been to recognise and observe all your positive personality strengths and virtuous beliefs about the world. This is *not* an angel in charge of producing self-criticism or blame!

One Small Step
For the next fifteen minutes, imagine that the angel is now dictating a list of your positive attributes through you. Writing down whatever comes to mind, make a list of what you think the angel would say.

Possibilities
Which personality traits do you value most and want to continue to influence your approach to life?
Which virtues or positive beliefs do you value most and want to continue to influence your approach to life?

Once you have done this exercise, take some time to contemplate what you wrote. This exercise is helpful for reclaiming and bolstering self-confidence and courage.

A Letter From The Future

One Small Step

Pick a time in the future (five, ten, fifteen or twenty years from now, or any length of time that is meaningful to you). Record the future date you have chosen at the head of your letter. Imagine that the intervening years have passed and you are writing to a close friend.

When writing the letter, imagine that you are living a joyous, healthy, satisfying life by the letter's date. If there are problems with which you are now struggling, assume that they have either been resolved, or that you have found satisfying ways to cope with them.

Explain how you resolved problems or difficulties that once plagued you. Describe how you did it, what you found to be most helpful from the vantage point of looking back on your life from the future.

Describe in detail how you spend your time in this imaginary future. Where are you living? Describe a typical day. Describe your relationships, beliefs, reflections on the past and speculations towards the more distant future.

This letter is not meant to be mailed. It is for you only. The purpose of dating the letter and writing it to a real person is to strengthen the psychological realism of the letter for you on both conscious and unconscious levels.

In writing your letter, don't worry about limiting yourself to things that seem realistic given your current life. This is not essential and may unnecessarily constrict you. The Letter from the Future should be written with an open heart and an open mind so that you have room to surprise yourself.

Creating A Symbol To Centre Yourself

 Possibilities
When in your life have you felt most relaxed, calm and centred?
Select one experience you would enjoy remembering in the future.
What was it about this experience that you found most relaxing
and meaningful? Notice which images, thoughts or words come to
mind.

 One Small Step
Now draw a picture or choose an object, photograph or quotation
that reminds you of that experience and that you can carry with
you in the future.

Use this symbol to centre, calm and replenish yourself when life
becomes stressful or when you simply want to relax.

THE HEART'S DESIRE COLLAGE

The Heart's Desire Collage will amplify your hopes and dreams. Giving them a tangible representation will also strengthen their presence in your unconscious.

Collect symbolic items ahead of time by assembling photographs, postcards, drawings or images from magazines that remind you of your heart's desires. Pieces of paper, leather or fabric in your favourite colours are also useful because these will evoke the positive feelings you associate with various shades and textures. You may also want to include objects from nature such as twigs, dried flowers or small shells. Don't forget your own drawings or paintings, and any special words that symbolise your hopes and dreams.

 One Small Step
Set aside at least an hour for this exercise. Where you spend this time is important. Make sure you have privacy or, if other people are around, that they are non-judgmental and supportive of what you are doing. You will need a piece of cardboard at least 8 by 10 inches, scissors, glue, writing or drawing implements and a collection of things that symbolise the hopes and dreams you began to explore when you wrote your Letter from the Future.

When making your collage, remember that the goal is to re-discover the free and childlike imagination of your Authentic Self. That means you are allowed to be playful and spontaneous, and it's fine to be messy. Don't be surprised if additional ideas occur to you while you're in the middle of making the collage.

The Last Fifteen Minutes Of The World

For this exercise you will need blank paper and writing or drawing implements.

Imagine that you have been gifted at birth with two things: the ability to express yourself well and some special knowledge to give the world. Unfortunately, you have not known of these abilities until now. You have also just learned that a terrible destructive force is about to hit the earth. This force will destroy all libraries, museums, computers and other information storage systems. Only those objects and information placed in a special time capsule will survive.

 One Small Step
You are asked to contribute to the time capsule. Write, draw or orally record your special information that will help the human race survive after the catastrophe. You have only fifteen minutes to do this.

Identifying ideas or thoughts deep within that you deem meaningful and important allows you to appreciate your unique knowledge and reflect it more fully in your daily life.

CREATING A NEW INFLUENCE FOR YOUR LIFE

 One Small Step

Think of someone who embodies a way of living that you value, a person you admire in some way. This person can be living or dead, famous or unknown. He or she can be someone you know personally, or someone you are acquainted with only through literature, films or stories you have heard. If at all possible, find a picture of this person (or draw one) to look at while you are doing this exercise.

Write a detailed description of this person, emphasising the qualities that you most admire.

Think about why you have chosen him or her to be an influence in your life.

 Possibilities

What do you find most appealing about this person's approach to life?

How would this person respond to your current situation?

Now that you have completed your Creating a New Influence exercise, the following questions will help you further integrate the positive qualities you identified into your own life.

 One Small Step

Think back to the person you chose as a new influence for your life.

 Possibilities

How are you like the person you described?

How are you different?

Which aspects of this person's lifestyle do you wish to incorporate into your life?

Are there any things that you are already doing that are examples of this? If so, what would be the effect of doing a little more of this in order to integrate this quality further into your personality? If not, what would be the first small step towards embodying their way of living?

If you don't believe you possess any of your chosen person's admirable qualities, what would be a small observable sign in your behaviour that would show that you were beginning to incorporate such qualities? Consider a scale of 1 to 10, in which 10 meant you had succeeded in incorporating a newly desired quality into your behaviour to the fullest degree possible, and 1 meant not at all.

What observable practice could you undertake that would raise your score half a point or more? Experiment with enacting the behaviour you identified, noticing the difference it makes for you. Then identify the next small step and try that, and so on. Report the results to the group.

A Tree That Speaks To You

This exercise needs to be done at a time of year when the group can walk around outdoors in a wooded setting.

The tree is a device upon which you can project your own thoughts, feelings and special awareness, thereby allowing your Authentic Self to speak to you.

 One Small Step

Give yourselves at least an hour to walk around and contemplate various trees. Look for a tree that you find particularly appealing. Imagine that this tree has something to tell you about your Authentic Self. Imagine that the tree knows something important about you because you are kindred spirits. Ask the tree to tell you how you are alike, and write down what comes to mind. Then ask the tree to tell you the message it has for you about your Authentic Self, and write down whatever you imagine the tree tells you.

Identifying with nature is another avenue for getting in touch more deeply with your Authentic Self.

A Time Line – Your Life Story

You will need paper and pencil for this exercise.

One Small Step

Draw a vertical line down the middle of a sheet of paper. On the upper left-hand corner write the word *birth* and your date of birth. Now list other information about yourself, such as approximate dates of starting school, moving, birth of siblings and so on, in chronological order. Add information as it comes to you, including both pleasant and unpleasant information that is significant to you.

Record past or current feelings about each event in the space across from it on the right-hand side of the vertical line.

One page will probably not be enough. You may think of additional information that needs to be inserted to retain the chronological order to your Time Line. Just cut the paper horizontally and use Sellotape and additional strips of paper to insert new text. You may continue to use paper and tape to form one long strip of paper that you can roll up and store in the form of a long scroll.

Discovering and exploring your life story is another way to deepen a connection with your Authentic Self.

A Coat Of Arms

If you were to create a Coat of Arms to represent your Authentic Self, which images would you include? Which colours best represent who you are? Would you include things that represent your accomplishments, your hobbies and other things you like to do? Is there a saying or a logo that you would include in the form of an inscription or a banner? Notice what comes to mind.

You will need blank paper; drawing, colouring or painting supplies; glue and some old magazines or newspapers.

One Small Step
Draw a Coat of Arms for yourself on a sheet of paper and notice what emerges. Feel free to add images cut out from newspapers and magazines, as well as objects from nature, such as discarded feathers, bits of dried wood or flowers. Remember that the idea in creating a Coat of Arms is to learn more about your Authentic Self. Don't worry if your creation is not great art!

This exercise will help you strengthen your self-confidence and positive self-identity.

A Rainy Day Letter

Ironically, when we most need comfort is when it's most difficult to remember. The Rainy Day letter will provide consolation when you most need it. Since a letter is portable, you can carry it with you to support you wherever you go. And it offers the wisdom of the person who knows you best: yourself!

 One Small Step
Set aside some time when you are calm and can relate this serenity to yourself at a future time when you are upset, overwhelmed or distressed. Write this letter from you to you.

1. List the activities that you find comforting
2. Write down the names and phone numbers of supportive friends or family members
3. Remind yourself of your strengths and virtues
4. Remind yourself of your special talents, abilities and interests
5. Remind yourself of your hopes and dreams for the future
6. Give yourself special advice or other reminders that are important to you.

You deserve the comfort your Rainy Day Letter will bring. Re-reading it and implementing some of the ideas it contains really can make a difference in times of stress and distress.

After writing your letter, read it aloud to the group or, if you prefer, simply describe what it was like to write your letter and how you plan to use it.

AN ANIMAL SYMBOL

If you could be any animal, what would you choose to be? Chances are
your choice says something about your Authentic Self.

 One Small Step
Draw a picture of this animal, then write a description of the
animal's special characteristics and habits. What qualities do you
find most appealing about this animal?

Now pretend that you are in fact the animal you have selected.
Take some time to imagine yourself as this animal. How would
you spend a typical day? What do you like and dislike about being
this animal?

This exercise will help you discover new alternatives for expressing
your various personality traits.

CHALLENGING THE PROSPERITY MIND-SET

Possibilities

What things do you associate with a pleasing, prosperous life?
What aspects of these things are more associated with behaviour or
personal style than with money?
Which are more dependent on money?
Can you give yourself some of these things now?
How might you use your personal creativity to facilitate this? What
would be the first small step?

While your list may contain things that only additional money could
buy, most people also list things that are not dependent on acquiring more
money. Once identified, at least some of the things you associate with
prosperity may well be within reach.

Figuring Out Who You Are
Apart From "Shoulds"

 One Small Step

If left unfettered, but nurtured and supported, how would you choose to pass your time? Notice what thoughts and images come to mind as you imagine this.

Possibilities

If you lived more in accord with your envisioned preferences rather than spending so much time on what you "should" do, what productive or useful things might occur in your life?

What is one small step you could take to initiate some of these newly discovered activities?

What small sign would show that you had begun to move in this direction?

Arrange to take this first small step and report the results back to the group.

A Symbol For The Time Of Your Life

This exercise will help you discover your own unique symbol to remind you to live fully and give priority to the things that really matter to you. Read the instructions completely before doing this exercise so that you won't have to interrupt yourself while in the middle of it.

 One Small Step

Find a comfortable place to sit where you will not be disturbed for the next fifteen minutes. Concentrate on your breathing until you achieve a comfortable state and feel centred in your body. Now close your eyes and gently ask your unconscious to give you a symbol that will remind you to spend your time in satisfying and heartfelt ways.

Sit quietly and notice what comes to mind after you ask yourself for a symbol. It may be an image, words or a feeling. Once you know what it is, write or draw it so that you will remember it in the future.

After the group meeting, place your symbol in a place where you will see it often.

Practicing Dying

The following exercise will help you shift into your own wise perspective about how to spend the time you have available in your life. Write your responses so that you can refer to them afterwards.

 One Small Step
Imagine that you have been told that you have only six months to live. Assume for the purposes of this exercise that although you have an incurable illness, thanks to the miracles of modern medicine you will remain relatively symptom-free and able to move around freely until the final moments of your life.

 Possibilities
How would you wish to spend the remaining months of your life?
Who are the people you would want to spend time with?
Which places would you like to visit or revisit?
Are there any specific things you would need to do to enhance a feeling of completion and peacefulness before you die?

Take a few moments now to examine your responses to the above questions; they are likely to hold valuable clues as to how you might best prioritise your time and more fully honour your most heartfelt longings and needs.

What would be the first small step you could take to incorporate these changes into your daily life? Now embark on this first project during the next week and report the results back to the group.

Rewriting Old Messages

 One Small Step

Consider which negative or destructive message from your past interferes with your confidence or positive feelings about your life. Now think of a new and healthy message you would like to receive instead. Write the new message repeatedly with each hand until it begins to feel like a familiar part of your belief system. Now share this new message with the group and have each group member say it to you while looking at you.

The impact of this new healthy message can be strengthened by writing it repeatedly after the group meeting. Don't worry if the positive message doesn't feel "real" or accurate the first few times you write it. As you continue to practice it, it will gradually begin to surface in your behaviour and the way you think about yourself and your life.

A Rainy Day Letter from the Group

When one member is leaving a group, a Rainy Day Letter from the Group is something she can carry with her after the last meeting and in the future.

 One Small Step
The person leaving the group starts a letter addressed to herself. Then she passes the letter around to the rest of the group. The other group members write messages of comfort and reassurance. Later she can reread the letter to reconnect to the feelings of support and validation she received from the group.

When a group is coming to a close, a Rainy Day Letter is something each member can take away after their last meeting.

 One Small Step
Each group member starts a letter addressed to herself. All the letters are passed around to each of the other members, who write messages of support or reassurance. Later each person can reread her letter to reconnect to the feelings of support or validation she received from the group.

A Rainy Day Letter is a good way to end a Small Steps Support Group. It also provides support and closure when someone is leaving the group.

Epilogue

It is time to share two things with you: a hope and a wish. My hope is that in the process of reading this book you have made use of the techniques that best fit for you, changing and adjusting them according to your own preferences and needs. Each time you have done that you have created something new, a unique expression of your Authentic Self that can serve as your own personal "candle" against the darkness of trauma and despair in the world.

My wish for you is a large one: May you experience all of life's blessings and great joy and satisfaction in your everyday life. You deserve nothing less.

Yvonne Dolan

BIBLIOGRAPHY

Bell-Gadsby, Chreyl and Siegenberg, Ann. (1995). Reclaiming Herstory: Ericksonian Solution-focused Therapy for Sexual Abuse. New York: Brunner-Mazel, 1995.

Berg, I.K. (1990). A solution-focused approach to family based services. Milwaukee, WI: Brief Family Therapy Center Publications.

Berg, I.K. & Miller, S. (1992). *Working With the Problem Drinker*. New York: Norton.

Berg, I.K. & de Shazer, S. (1993). Making numbers talk: Language in Therapy. In S. Friedman (Ed.), *The New Language of Change: Constructive Collaboration in Psychotherapy* (pp.5-24). New York: Guilford.

Berg, I.K. (1995). "So What Else is Better? Solutions for Substance Abuse." (videotape). Milwaukee, WI: Brief Family Therapy Center.

Bolen, Jean Shinoda. (1994). *Crossing to Avalon: A Woman's Midlife Pilgrimage*. San Francisco: HarperSanFrancisco, 1994.

Breathnach, S.B. (1995). *Simple Abundance: A Daybook of Comfort and Joy*. New York: Warner.

Bristol, C. (1948). *The Magic of Believing*. New York: Simon & Schuster.

Cameron, Julia. (1992). *The Artist's Way: A Spiritual Path to Higher Creativity*. New York: Tarcher.

Combs, G. & Freedman, J. *The Social Construction of Preferred Realities*. (1996). New York: Norton.

Csikszentmihalyi, M. (1990). *Flow: The Psychology of Optimal Experience*. New York: Harper Collins.

de Shazer, S. (1982). *Patterns of Brief Family Therapy*. New York: Guilford.

de Shazer, S. (1985). *Keys to Solution in Brief Therapy*. New York: Norton.

de Shazer, S. (1988). *Clues to Investigation in Brief Family Therapy*. New York: Norton.

de Shazer, S. (1991). *Putting Difference to Work*. New York: Norton.

de Shazer, S. (1994). *Words Were Originally Magic*. New York: Norton.

Dolan, Y. (1985). *A Path With a Heart: Ericksonian Utilization with Resistant and Chronic Clients*. New York: Brunner-Mazel.

Dolan, Y. (1991). *Resolving Sexual Abuse: Solution-focused Therapy and*

Ericksonian Hypnosis With Adult Survivors. New York: Norton.

Dolan, Y. (1994). Solution-focused therapy with a case of severe abuse. In M.F. Hoyt (Ed.), *Constructive Therapies* (pp.276-294). New York: Guilford.

Dolan, Y. (1994b). An Ericksonian perspective on the treatment of sexual abuse. In J.K. Zeig (Ed.) *Ericksonian Methods: The Essence of the Story.* New York: Guilford.

Erickson, Milton H. (1959). "Further Techniques of Hypnosis: Utilization Techniques." *American Journal of Clinical Hypnosis,* 1: 3-21.

Erickson, Milton H. (1958). "Naturalistic Techniques of Hypnosis: Utilization Techniques. " *American Journal of Clincal Hypnosis.* 1: 3-8.

Erickson, Milton H. (1965). "The Use of Symptoms As an Integral Part of Therapy." *American Journal of Clinical Hypnosis,* 1: 198-209.

Erickson, Milton H. Rossi, Ernest L., & Rossi, Sheila K. (1976). *Hypnotic Realities.* New York: Irvington.

Estes, Clarissa Pinkola. (1992). *Women Who Run with the Wolves: Myths and Stories of the Wild Woman Archetype.* New York: Ballantine.

Field, Joanna.(1981). *A Life of One's Own.* New York: Tarcher.

Furman, B. & Ahola, T. (1992), *Solution Talk: Hosting the therapeutic conversation.* New York: Norton.

George, Evan & Iveson, Chris & Ratner, Harvey. (1999, new edition). *Problem to Solution: Brief Therapy with Individuals and Families.* London: B T Press.

Gilligan, S. (1997). *The Courage to Love: Principles and Practices of Self Relations Psychotherapy.* New York: Norton.

Haley, Jay & Richeport, Madeline. *Milton H. Erickson, MD: Explorer in Hypnosis and Therapy.* Rockville, MD: Triangle Productions Videotape.

Holzer, Nina Burghild. (1994). *A Walk Between Heaven and Earth.* New York: Bell Tower.

Iveson, Chris. (1990). *Whose Life? Community Care of Older People and Their Families.* London: B T Press.

Jung, Carl Gustav. (1965). *Memories, Dreams, Reflections.* New York: Vintage.

Kerr, Michael & Bowen, Murray. (1988). *Family Evaluation: An Approach Based on Bowen Theory.* New York: Norton.

Lethem, Jane. (1994). *Moved to Tears, Moved to Action: Solution-focused Brief Therapy with Women and Children.* London: B T Press.

Lipchik, Eve. (1988). "Purposeful Sequences for Beginning the Solution-Focused Interview." In Interviewing edited by Eve Lipchik, 105-117. Rockville, MD: Aspen.

Livingston, Angela. (1984). *Salome: Her Life and Works.* London: Gordon Fraser.

Louden, Jennifer. (1992). *The Woman's Comfort Book.* San Fransico: Harper.

Metzger, Deanna. (1992). *Writing Your Life: A Guide and Companion to the*

Inner Worlds. San Francisco: Harper.

Miller, Gale. (1997). *Becoming Miracle Workers*. New York: Aldine de Gruyter.

Mitchell, Stephen. (1993). *The Gospel According to Jesus. A New Translation Guide to His Essential Teachings for Believers and Non-Believers*. New York: HarperCollins.

Mitchell, Stephen. ed. (1993). *The Enlightened Mind: An Anthology of Sacred Prose*. New York: HarperPerennial.

Napier, N. (1997). *Sacred Practices for Conscious Living*. New York: Norton.

Nash, Ogden. (1938). *I'm a Stranger Here Myself*. Boston: Little, Brown and Company.

Neruda, Pablo.(1994). English translation by Kenneth Krabbenhoft, *Odes to Opposites*. Boston: Little, Brown, and Company.

O'Hanlon, B. & Weiner-Davis, M. (1989). *In Search of Solutions*. New York: Norton.

Parker, Dorothy W. (1994). *The Poems and Short Stories of Dorothy Parker*. New York: Random House.

Rechtschaffen, S. (1996). *Time Shifting: Creating More Time to Enjoy Your Life*. New York: Doubleday.

Redman, Alvin. ed. (1959). *The Wit and Humor of Oscar Wilde*. New York: Dover.

Rossi, E.L., Rossi, K.L. (Ed.), (1996) *The Symptom Path to Enlightenment: The New Dynamics of Self-Organization in Hypnotherapy, An Advanced Manual for Beginners*. Pacific Palisades, CA: Gateway.

Rossi, E.L. (1991). *The 20 Minute Break*. Los Angeles: Tarcher.

Saine, Thomas P. and Sammons, Jeffrey, eds. (1987). *Goethe: The Collected Works*, Vol. 4. Princeton, New Jersey: Princeton University Press.

Sarton, May. (1973). *Journal of a Solitude*. New York: Norton.

Schnarch, D. (1997). *Passionate Marriage*. New York: Norton.

Shaughnessy, Susan. (1993). *Walking on Alligators: A Book of Meditations for Writers*. San Francisco: Harper.

St. James, E. (1995). *Inner Simplicity: 100 Ways to Regain Peace and Nourish Your Soul*. New York: Hyperion.

Synder, M. & White, P. (1982). Moods, memories: elation, depression, and the remembering of the events of one's life. Journal of Personality. 50 (2): 149-167.

Too, Lillian. (1996). *The Complete Illustrated Guide to Feng Shui: How to Apply the Secrets of Chinese Wisdom for Health, Wealth, and Happiness*. London: Element Publishers.

Walters, C. & Havens, R. (1993). *Hypnotherapy for Health, Harmony, and Peak Performance: Expanding the Goals of Hypnotherapy*. New York: Brunner/Mazel.

Wapnick, Kenneth. From a talk given on A Course in Miracles. Roscoe,

New York: Foundation for A Course in Miracles.

Weiner-Davis, Michelle. (1992). *Divorce Busting: A Revolutionary and Rapid Program for Staying Together*. New York: Simon & Schuster.

Wells, Rebecca. (1996). *Divine Secrets of the Ya-Ya Sisterhood*. New York: HarperCollins.

Wolinsky, S. (1996). *Hearts on Fire: The Tao of Meditation*. San Diego: Blue Dove Press.